TOBI KAHN

METAMORPHOSES

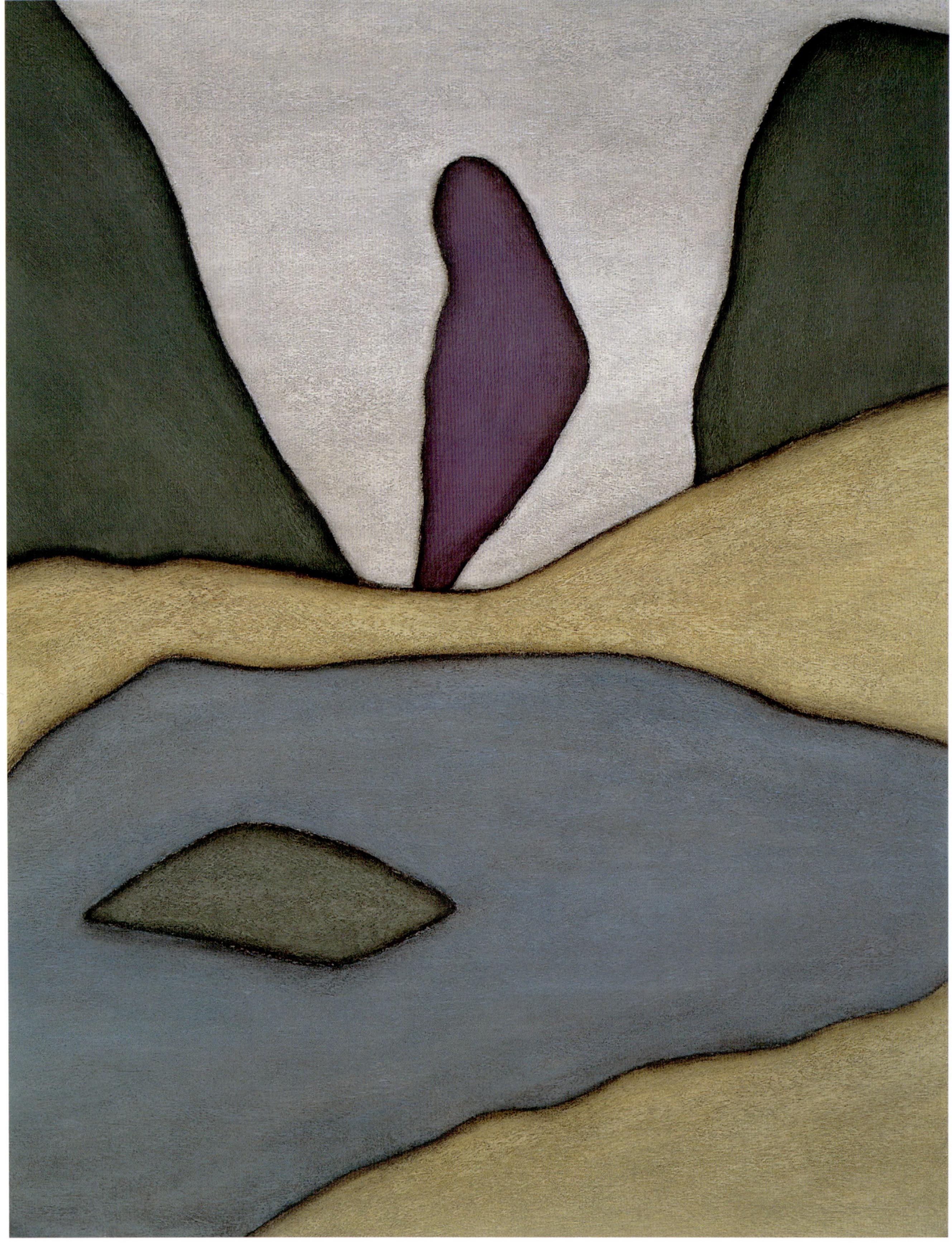

TOBI KAHN

METAMORPHOSES

Curated by Peter Selz

Essays by Peter Selz, Dore Ashton, Michael Brenson

Published by the Council for Creative Projects

Distributed by the University of Washington Press

EXHIBITION ITINERARY

Weatherspoon Art Gallery
The University of North Carolina at Greensboro
August 3 – October 26, 1997

The Trout Gallery
Dickinson College, Carlisle, Pennsylvania
November 18, 1997 – January 24, 1998

Museum of Contemporary Religious Art
Saint Louis University, St. Louis, Missouri
March 6 – May 8, 1998

Thomas J. Walsh Art Gallery
Regina A. Quick Center for the Arts at
Fairfield University, Fairfield, Connecticut
June 5 – July 16, 1998

Colby College Museum of Art
Waterville, Maine
August 12 – October 11, 1998

The Museum of Fine Arts
Houston, Texas
November 8, 1998 – January 31, 1999

Judah L. Magnes Museum and Graduate Theological Union
Berkeley, California
March 3 – May 23, 1999

Skirball Cultural Center and Museum
Los Angeles, California
June 17 – August 26, 1999

This catalogue has been published with the generous support of
the Robert Lee Blaffer Trust; Mitchell Investment Management
Company, Inc.; The Green Fund; Swiss Bank Corporation;
Hambro-Spinner Renaissance Fund; Armin and Ann C. Kessler;
Charles A. and Ilana Horowitz Ratner; Rose and Morton Landowne;
Tracey and Mark Bilski; Clyde Hershan; Sybil and Arthur Levine;
and other funders.

Contents

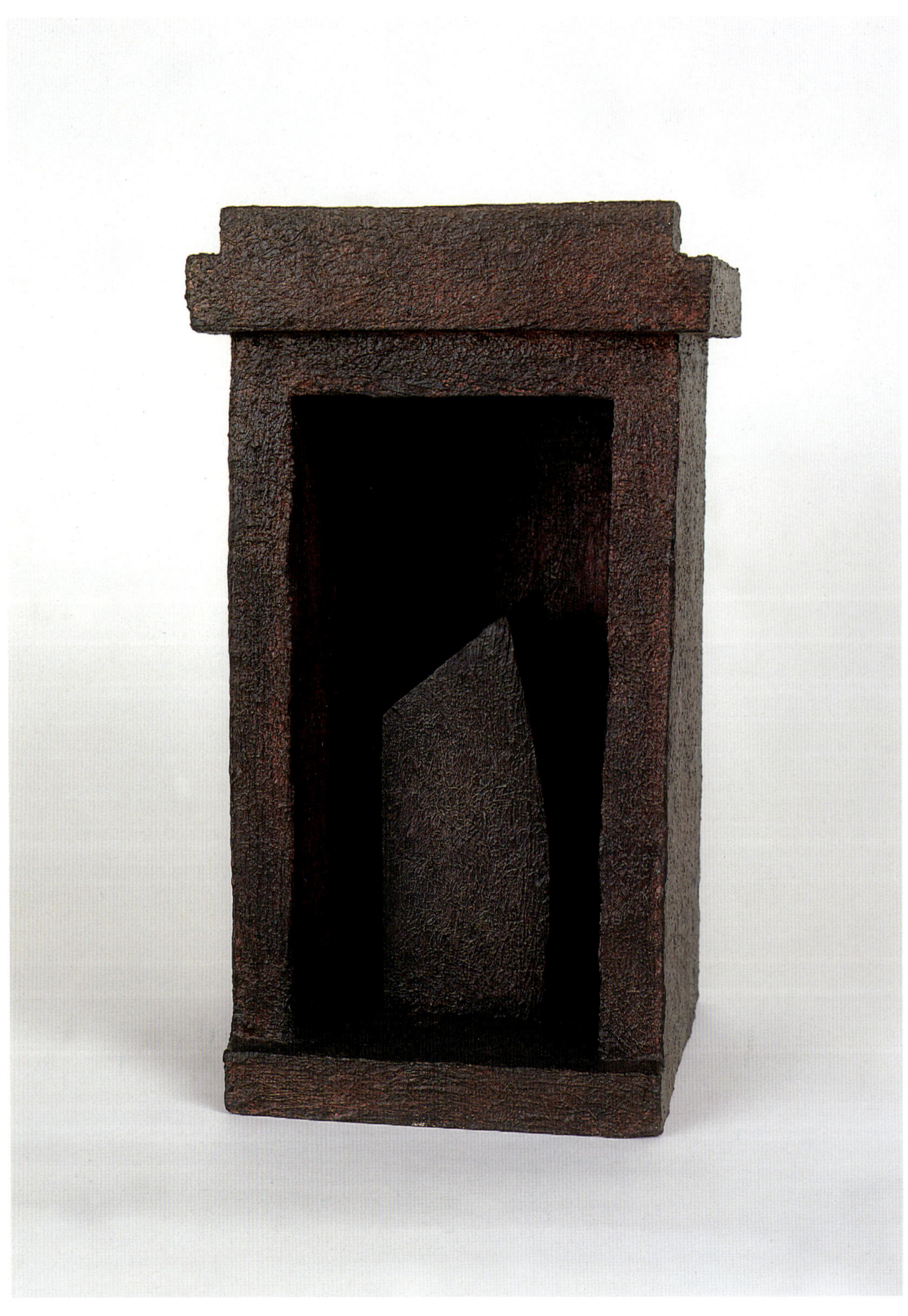

ACKNOWLEDGMENTS

It is a distinct pleasure to be able to publish this volume as a contribution to the critical literature on Tobi Kahn. It must be noted that without the tremendous support and effort of many people, this project would not have been possible. First and foremost, the Council for Creative Projects would like to thank Peter Selz, who brought Kahn's work to our attention and has now meticulously curated this exhibition. We are also grateful to Dore Ashton and Michael Brenson for agreeing to contribute their insights to this catalogue. We want to thank Joel Meyers for his unflagging dedication in coordinating the exhibition tour; Carol Bosco for her curatorial and publication assistance and her commitment to assuring that the individual works are safe and accessible through a melange of educational programming; and Gretchen Kettenhofen, who organized and assisted with the development and funding program. We are grateful to Dino Alberto, Joel Haffner, Nils Karsten and James Lorey, Kahn's studio assistants, who were scrupulous in following up on every detail.

For creating this beautiful book we would like to thank Elizabeth Finger for the design, and Sharon Florin and Nessa Rapoport for their precision in editing the text. We are grateful to numerous institutions and individuals for their generous support of this project. They include: The Robert Lee Blaffer Trust, Mitchell Investment Management Company, Inc., The Green Fund, Swiss Bank Corporation, Hambro-Spinner Renaissance Fund, Armin and Ann C. Kessler, Charles A. and Ilana Horowitz Ratner, Tracey and Mark Bilski, Rose and Morton Landowne, Clyde Hershan, Sybil and Arthur Levine, and other funders.

This exhibition could not have taken place without the lenders, who graciously agreed to share the art in their collections; and the institutions participating in the exhibition tour, whose cooperation and enthusiasm were essential to the successful completion of this project.

A special note of thanks is reserved for Douglas Dreishpoon, Curator of Collections at the Weatherspoon Art Gallery, University of North Carolina at Greensboro. The institution not only begins the tour, but he has personally assisted in every aspect of the development of the exhibition and catalogue. His insights and expertise were invaluable.

In the end, this exhibition and catalogue are a tribute to the aesthetic vision of Tobi Kahn. A comprehensive exhibition of this caliber could not have been achieved without the artist's unrelenting assistance. On behalf of Tobi Kahn, then, we would also like to thank Nessa, Josh, Mattie, Ellen and Herbert Kahn, as well as all the friends who gave guidance and encouragement to this project.

Gail Gelburd, Ph.D.
Executive Director
Council for Creative Projects

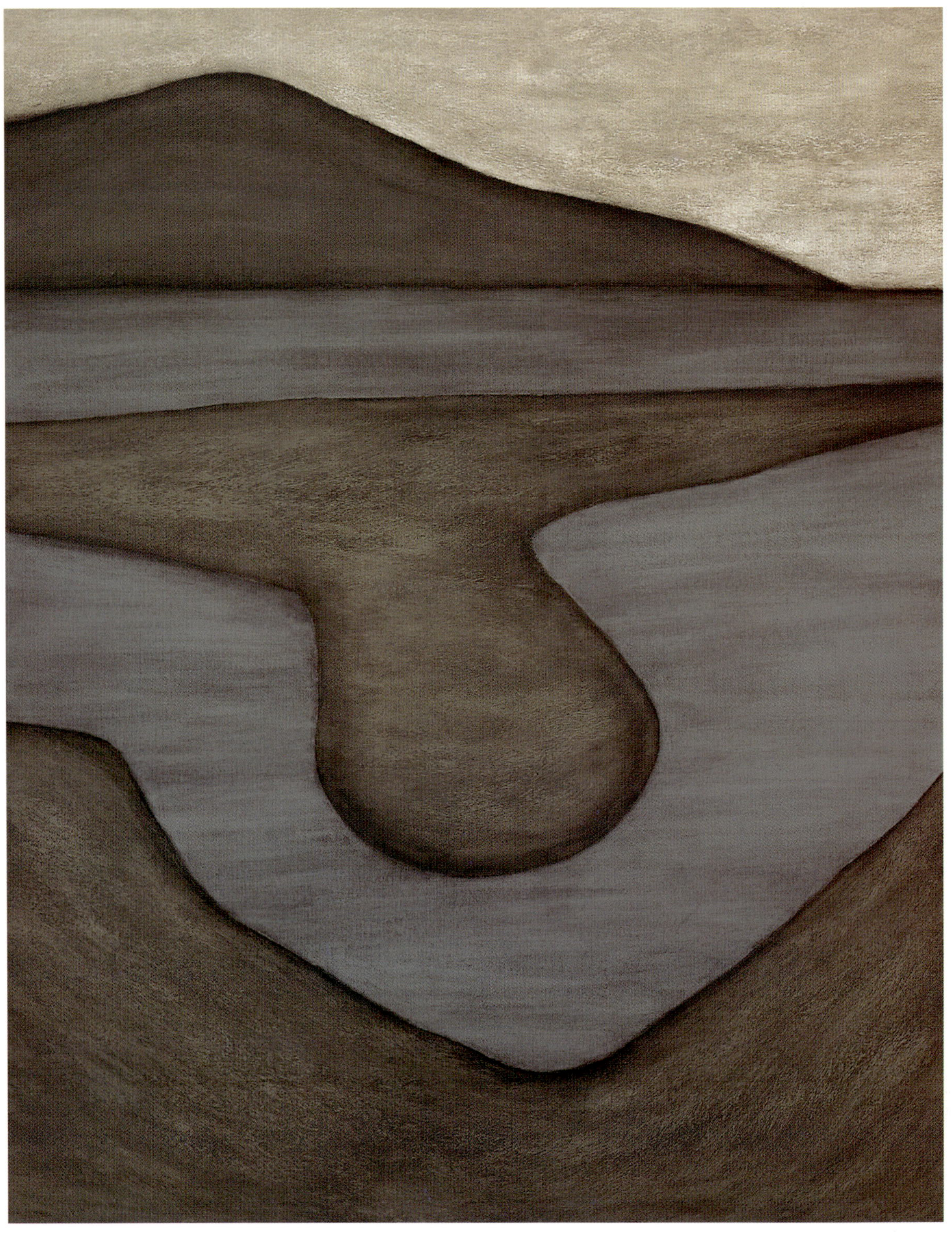

Lenders to the Exhibition

Colby College Museum of Art, Waterville, Maine

Georgene S. and Irving H. Dreishpoon

Arlene and Howard Eisenberg

Karen Lehmann Eisner and David F. Eisner

Solomon R. Guggenheim Museum, New York

Clyde Hershan

Andrea and Robert Hershan

The Jewish Museum, New York

Ellen and Herbert Kahn

Josh R. Kahn and Mattie R. Kahn

Leonard A. Kestenbaum

Rose and Morton Landowne

Elysa Lazar

Douglas F. Maxwell

Mitchell Investment Management Company, Inc.

Museum of Contemporary Religious Art, St. Louis, Missouri

New Amsterdam Brewing Company

Drs. Bonnie Maslin and Yehuda Nir

Private Collections

Nessa Rapoport

Idee German Schoenheimer

Hilde and Sidney Schonfeld

Sunrise Financial Group, Inc.

Swiss Bank Corporation

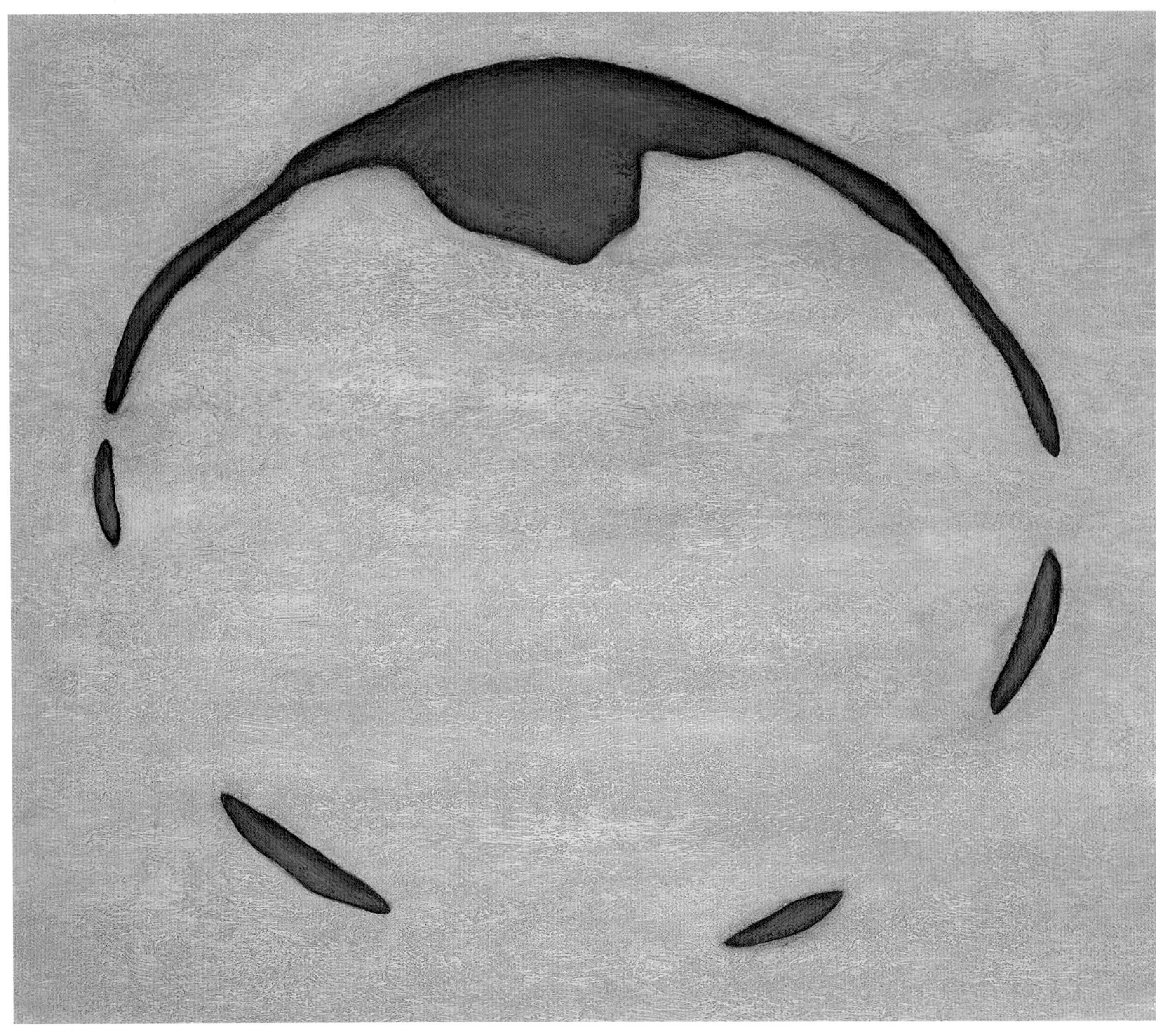

Tobi Kahn: Metamorphoses

PETER SELZ

The earth does not argue
It is not pathetic, has no arrangements
Does not scream, haste, persuade, threaten, promise
Makes no discrimination, has no conceivable failures,
Closes nothing, refuses nothing, shuts none out,
Of all the powers, objects, states, it notifies, shuts none out.

WALT WHITMAN

A SONG OF THE ROLLING EARTH

The Romantics believed in a pantheist unity of all aspects of the universe, striving to set aside distinctions between subject and object — the self and things — and to immerse themselves into a cosmic and numinous totality. Romantic landscape painters, such as Casper David Friedrich, would observe their response to nature as an aspect of a transcendental unity. Friedrich advised artists to "shut their physical eyes in order to first see the picture with their spiritual eye."[1] Intimacy with nature and a true understanding of its meaning precludes its imitation for the Romantic artist, because, as Baudelaire summarized: "Romanticism is precisely situated neither in choice of subject nor in exact truth, but in a *mode of feeling.*"[2]

The Romantics — painters, poets, thinkers — meditated on the inner life of appearances, on the emotions aroused by the sea, the meadow, the mountain or the cloud. In America it was in the work of the Luminist painters, such as John F. Kensett, Fitz Hugh Lane and Martin J. Heade, that we notice this attitude of the artist's intuitive expression of feelings vis-a-vis the landscape, a subjective fusion of the real and the ideal. Based on Emerson's transcendental philosophy, which saw the divinity immersed in the forms of nature, the Luminists conveyed a detached serenity and an emanation of mysterious light, which may very well have been intended to reveal spiritual sentiments.[3]

Albert Pinkham Ryder continued the American Romantic tradition by inventing moonlit seascapes with lonely boats under dark, turbulent skies — seascapes that relate to Wagnerian mythology rather than to direct optical observation. Tobi Kahn, who speaks of Ryder with admiration, does not share the latter's predilection for Gothic scenes, but also explores dreams, memories and myth in his paintings; he shares Ryder's process of elaborate layering of pigments as well as his sense of rhythmic pattern.

A few years after Ryder died, Marsden Hartley pointed out that "Ryder was the last of the romantics, the last of that great school of impressive artists, as he was the first of our real painters and the greatest in vision.... He was the painter poet of the immanent in things."[4] Hartley, another painter who can be seen as antecedent to Kahn, painted at the end of his life somber, dark Ryderesque pictures of monumental silence, based on his visions of the land, sea and mountains of his "native continent of Maine."

The artists of the Stieglitz Circle — Hartley and Marin, Dove and O'Keeffe — were able to penetrate the mystery of the American land by structuring their subjective visions into ordered formal compositions, which, it appears to me, is the goal of Kahn's own work in painting and sculpture. Perhaps closest among his forebears is the work of Arthur G. Dove. Dove, America's first abstract painter, knew how to make the invisible visible. He perceived the world around him — earth, water and snow, flowers and trees, sun and moon and the sound of the foghorns in Long Island Sound — and responded with paintings of harmonious peace. During the 1920s, he also reached beyond the limitations of the picture plane and constructed assemblages. His friend, the poet William Carlos Williams, once exclaimed: "Not ideas, but things," and Arthur Dove called his three-dimensional objects "things." He would appropriate discarded materials for these assemblages and then put them together to yield metaphorical meanings.

Dove clearly also enjoyed the palpable "thingness," the careful construction of these works, as Tobi Kahn, another artist-builder, does in his finely crafted objects. Over the years he has carved originally conceived furniture; he has crafted Jewish ceremonial objects — menorahs, carvings on Torah arks, candlesticks and chalices. During his earlier years as a painter, he also built his own wooden frames to give a greater sense of physical presence to his paintings, and since the late 1970s, he has created small shrines. At first he assembled all kinds of discarded and found throwaways with a history of their own and combined them into new pieces. But soon he started to fashion ritualistic objects that enshrined single bronze humanoid figures. These resemble the small terra-cotta models of Greco-Roman temples, as well as reliquaries of the Judeo-Christian tradition.

It was at the 1987 exhibition *Sacred Spaces*, at the Everson Museum in Syracuse, New York, that I first encountered the work of Tobi Kahn. This important exhibition, following the large review of modern abstract art, *The Spiritual in Art: Abstract Painting 1890–1985*, mounted at the Los Angeles County Museum earlier that year, clarified much of the thinking and criticism of modernist art. It became evident that

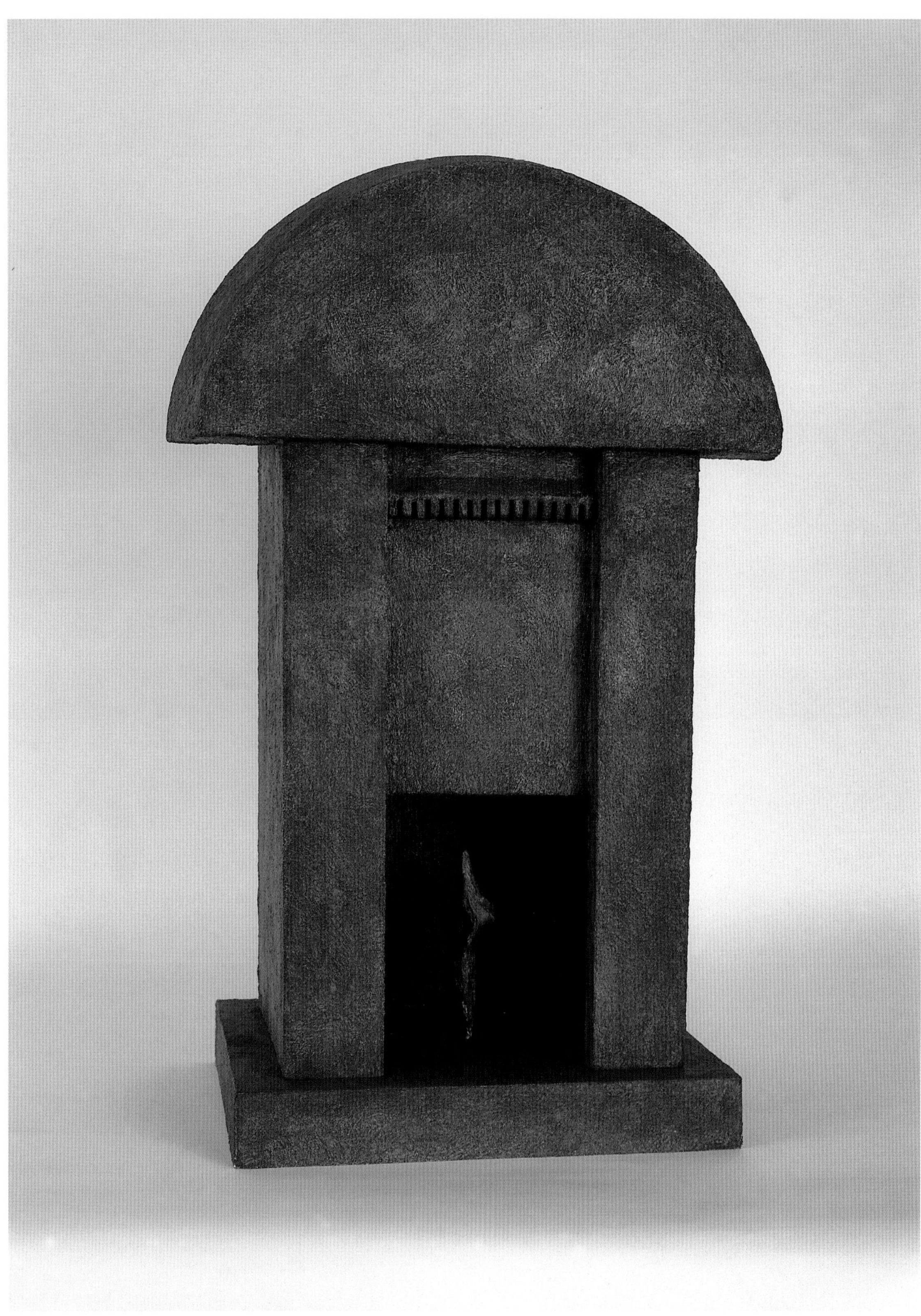

the widespread idea, shared by Formalist and Marxist critics, that modern art, located in secular culture, separated itself from the realm of the spirit, was only a part of the truth. While totally rejecting the repetitive pious church art, many modern artists created art that affirmed a spiritual perception of ultimacy and universality. The great pioneers of abstraction were involved with Theosophist teachings in the period prior to World War I. Kandinsky spoke about "harkening to the inner sound" in his treatise entitled *On the Spiritual in Art*; Malevich spoke of a "Suprematist search for God"; and Mondrian affirmed that a new, Neo-Plastic art would ascend from reality to abstraction to approach the spirit. Such concerns are also evident in the silent black paintings by Ad Reinhardt; in Mark Rothko's tragic evocative panels; in Barnett Newman's sublime "Stations of the Cross"; and in the paintings by Agnes Martin, who speaks of beauty as producing transcendental response, and whose persona and work continue to be a great inspiration to Tobi Kahn.

Kahn's small wood altars are clearly objects of spiritual significance, as he explains: "When I conceived this series of sculptures in 1978, I was fascinated by the depiction in Leviticus of the Holy of Holies, a space within a space that housed a sacred object in its innermost chamber. Throughout my travels I noticed that it was the space surrounding the sacred object in various cultures that interested me. In these sculptures I try to replicate the aura of a chosen object in communion with its own constructed space."[5]

In an article I wrote in response to the Syracuse exhibition,[6] I commented on the feeling of closure suggested by *Brun* (1985), a small sanctuary that was painted in layers of orange pigment. The enclosure, with its welcoming surface, envelops a humanoid figure in its own black space. Another shrine, *Ziba II* (1987), has the shape of a tall, narrow cabinet with a much larger hanging bronze figure that could also be read as a bone or a sacred relic, depending on the viewer's subliminal images and expectations. *Brun, Ziba*, in fact all the titles of Kahn's work, are words that he makes up. This is to elicit free association, as none of his pieces are meant to be descriptive or narrative, and the title "Untitled" became a bore some time ago.

The size, but not the scale, of the shrines was kept intimate until 1993, when Jane Blaffer Owen commissioned a large granite-and-bronze outdoor sculpture by Kahn to stand on a field outside the town of New Harmony, Indiana. It was in New Harmony that Robert Owen, in the early 19th century, created a community devoted to utopian socialism. By the mid-20th century, however, it had become almost a ghost town until it was revived by Jane Owen as a center of humanist seminars and a site for modern architecture—with Philip Johnson's roofless church, Richard Meier's community building, and sculptures by Jacques Lipchitz, Stephen De Staebler, as well as Tobi Kahn. The latter's *Shalev*, a 12½ foot granite gateway, stands in fields of buffalo grass near the Wabash River on the outskirts of the town. The fields flood once a year, creating a

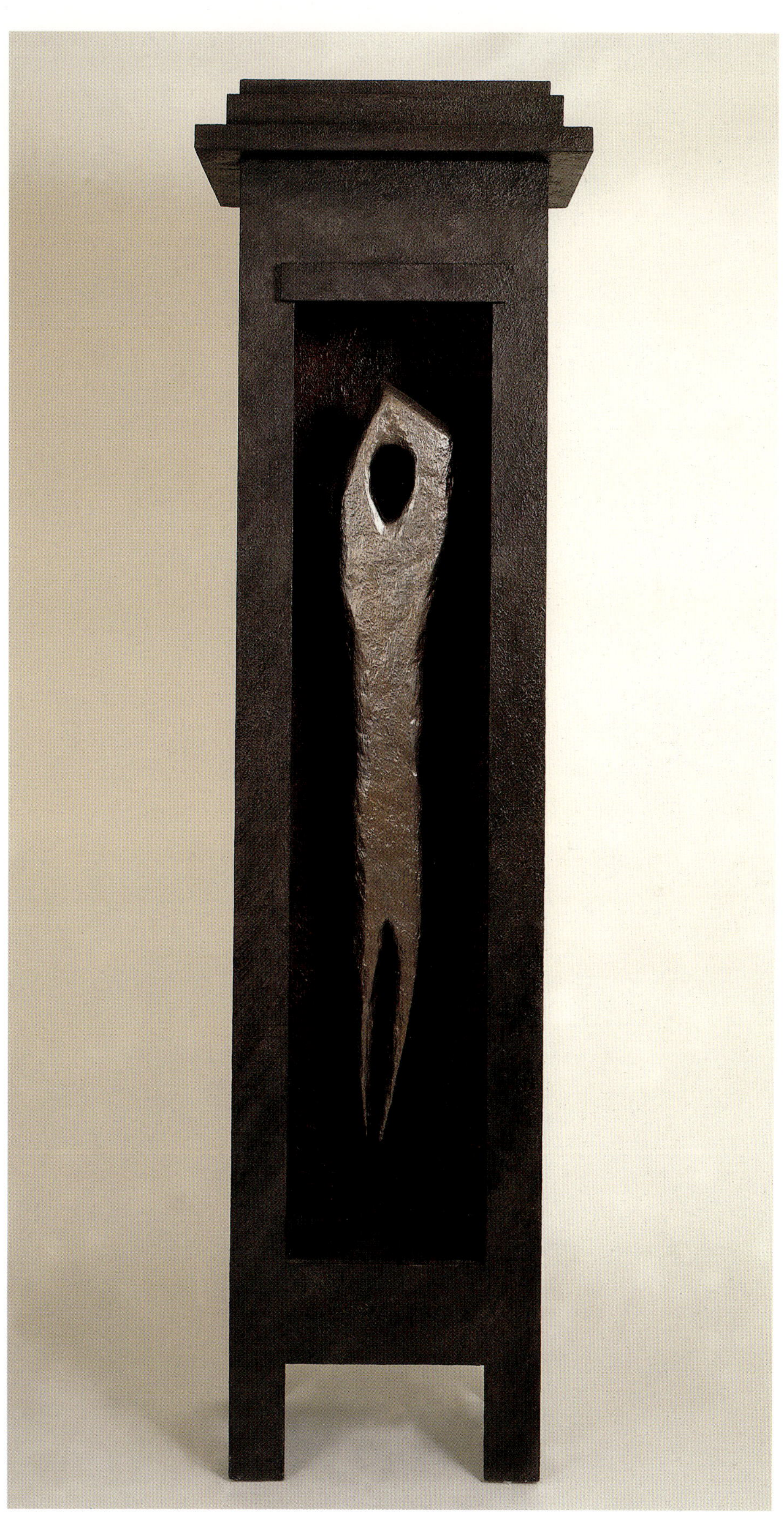

Granite exterior: 150 x 98 x 44 inches
Bronze interior: 60 x 20 x 14 inches
New Harmony, Indiana

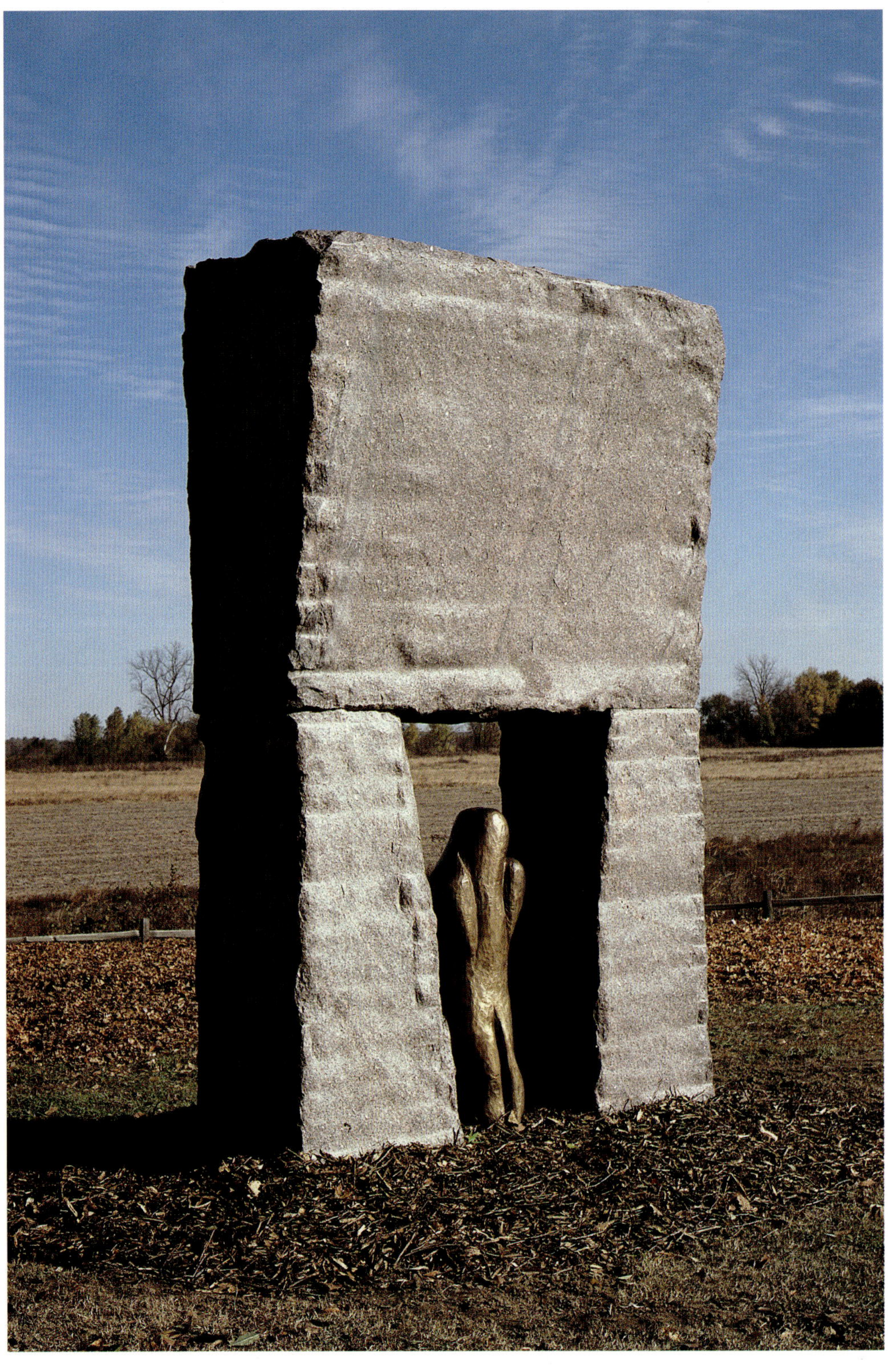

shallow lake close to the sculpture. Like the Neolithic dolmens in the landscape of England and Brittany that marked noteworthy spaces in the land, *Shalev* rises from the soil toward the sky. On moonlit nights the mica chips in the granite respond with sparks of light and create a sense of mystery, enhanced by the ambiguous figure, or figures, of embracing lovers inside the rectangular archway. "Within the name *Shalev* are intimations of words for "peace, tranquillity and heart." The sculpture's name amply reflects my intention."[7]

Among Kahn's major works in three dimensions are also stage designs, such as the huge rib cage for *Jonah* at the New York Public Theatre in 1990. At the time of this writing, Tobi Kahn is working on a Holocaust memorial, *Gan Hazikaron: Garden of Remembrance*, in Tenafly, New Jersey, which will consist of five bronzes, archetypal forms set in a wooded rock garden. These abstract figures, signifying the artist's tribute to the victims of the Shoah, will remain ambiguous enough for each viewer to construe his/her meaning in individual ways. They evoke, as the sculptor writes, "the interlude between memory and imagination that is yours alone, provoked by this circular common space."[8] It is appropriate that Tobi Kahn, some of whose German-Jewish family members were murdered in the camps, was commissioned to create this sanctuary.

Tobi Kahn was initially trained as a photographer at Hunter College, where he received his B.A. in 1976. His first exhibition, *Wall Fragments*, at Fordham University in 1979, consisted of photographs of walls impregnated by time that he saw in the South Bronx, as well as during his extensive travels to Scandinavia, Greece, Italy, the Middle East, and Africa. He was fascinated by the textures of the defaced, marked, peeling ancient walls and recorded their surfaces with his camera. Unlike Brassaï or Aaron Siskind, who did not touch or retouch what they had selected, Kahn, the incipient painter, would often add lines or shading to the walls, before photographing them, to complete his vision. In addition, he would make small, wood-backed paintings of walls on canvas or on sandpaper. These pieces were explorations of patterns, textures, surfaces, and their evocative possibilities.

In 1978, he completed his formal education at Pratt Institute, where he found George McNeil's teaching of special value. McNeil had participated in the important art movements of his time in New York. He was one of the founders of the American Abstract Artists group, painted originally in a geometric abstract style, and then became a member of the first generation of Abstract Expressionists in the 1940s. As time went on, the figure made a central appearance in McNeil's paintings, which suggested the work of the CoBrA artists; and Tobi Kahn's early paintings are experiments in figurative painting, as exemplified by *Ishon* (1977) (fig. 1), a head with a troubled, pensive expression of vulnerability. It was done in encaustic on collaged paper, already showing the artist's love for engaging with materials. A year later, he applied the encaustic in a pure

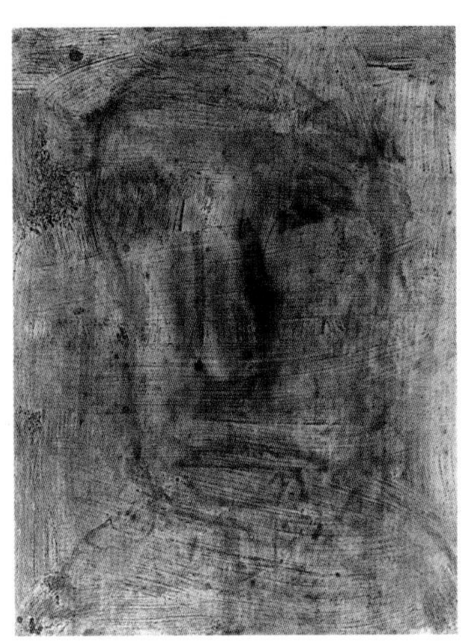

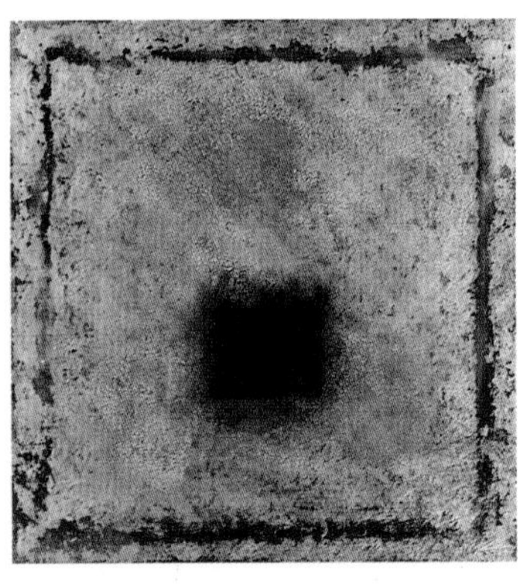

abstraction, *Tamh* (1979) (fig. 2). Here a dark black square is the focus of a grey square surface, with a dark line outlining its border. This was a time of exploration for the young artist, who was acutely aware of the masters of the previous generation, from Dubuffet and Golub to Rothko and Newman. The period of experimentation continued with a series of white-on-white paintings recalling Agnes Martin and Robert Ryman, black-on-black paintings, and then pictures that were related to the so-called "New Image Painting" by artists such as Robert Moskowitz and Susan Rothenberg.

By around 1984, the landscape as reflected in memory becomes the dominant theme of Kahn's mature work. A painting like *Iza II* (1984) indicates the main direction of his work as a painter. There are free-floating forms whose shapes and color suggest archetypal landscapes, which can be seen simultaneously as mindscapes of the artist's imagination. They clearly indicate that the old dispute between abstraction and figuration was a matter of the distant past, as the dominant dark triangular shapes suggest mountains, a lake or river, and a grey sky. The chalky surface, the interlocking forms and close-valued hues convey a quiescent memory. In these early paintings the artist developed a unique technique that—with certain alterations—he has used for more than a decade.

He begins by making a graphite drawing and then transfers the image in charcoal to a surface prepared with layers of gesso sanded to a smooth finish. Smaller works are usually painted on birch plywood; larger ones are painted on canvas stretched over a thinner, more portable wood support. In the next stage he paints the image in black and white to see the composition.

Then modeling paste is applied as the base ground of the image, which is built up with layers of powdered pigment dissolved in acrylic polymer medium. The bottom layers are generally opaque, whereas the subsequent layers tend to be more translucent through the use of washes. The work's luminous character is achieved through subtle variations of paint and wash. Some of Kahn's pictures are noticeably dense. One result of this labor-intensive process is that the viewer observing a specific area of a painting may apprehend different hues, depending on the angle of vision and the direction of light.

The importance of the psychological impact of color in Kahn's painting was well articulated by Lisa Dennison, the curator of the Guggenheim Museum's landmark 1985 exhibition, *New Horizons in American Art.*

> *The manipulation of color for Kahn is a deliberate and thoughtful process; the extensive power and poetry of the paintings emanate first and foremost from the gentle pulsation of his exquisite close-valued hues.... Though there is no discernible light source in Kahn's work, there is a magical luminosity that emanates from the white ground and is enhanced by the delicate translucency of his veils of color.*[9]

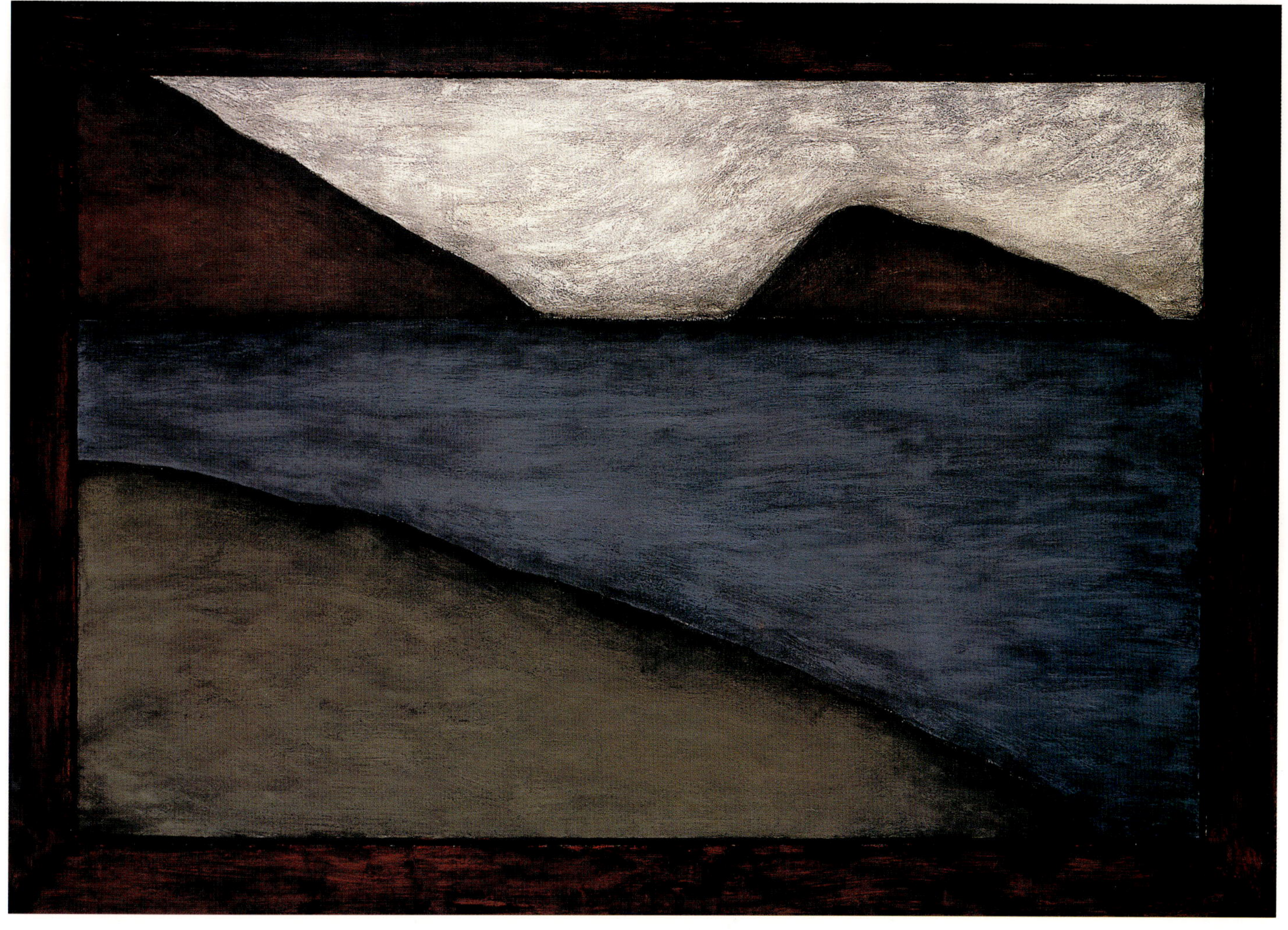

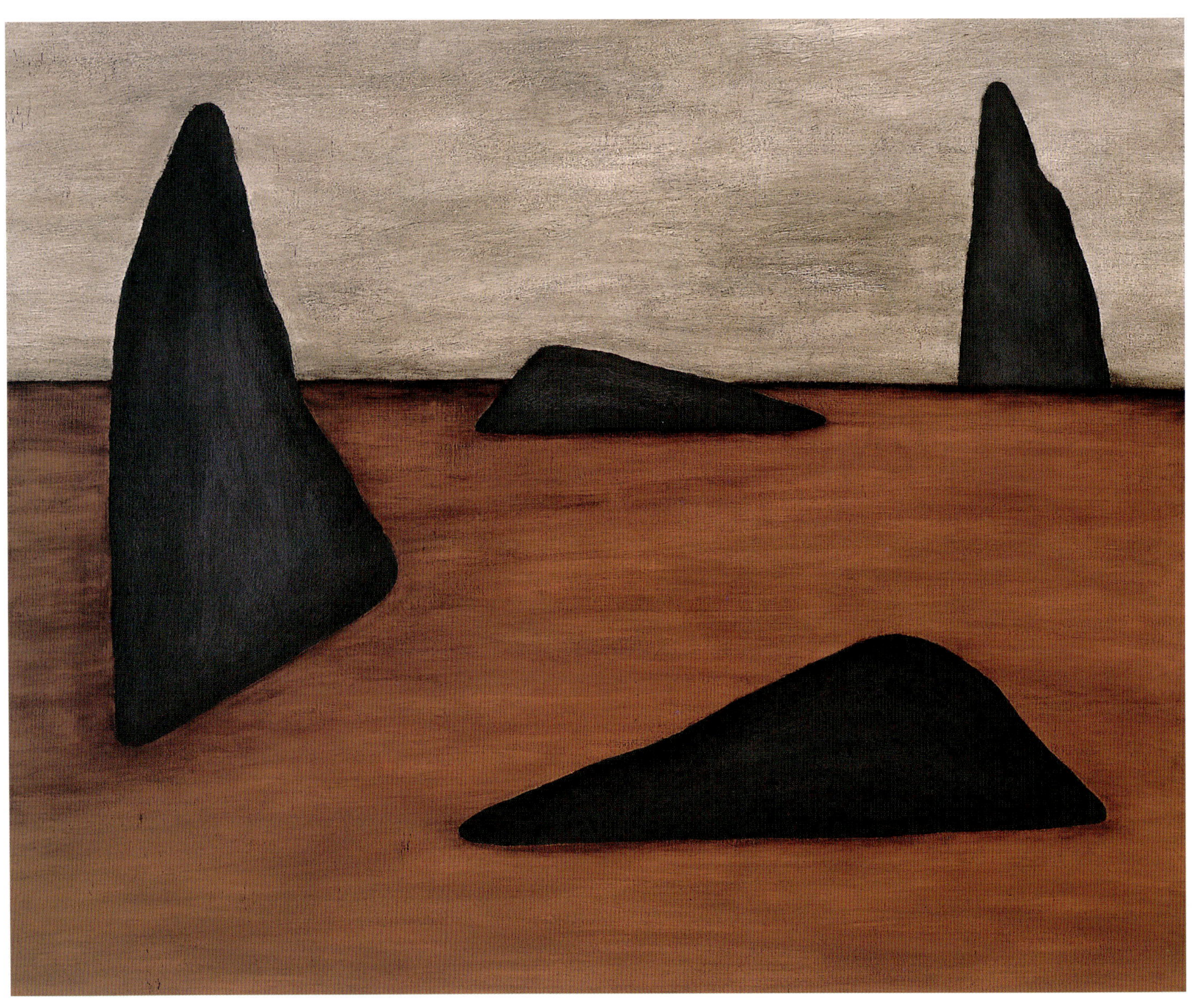

Kahn spent the summer of 1985 in Jerusalem, with many visits to the desert. Although a picture like *Giro III* does not suggest a desert landscape to most viewers, it is the result of his experience of "a world reduced to its necessary forms and bleached in blinding light. In the purity of that light, the soul can dream."[10]

If a sense of calm can be derived from seeing paintings like *Iza II* or *Giro III* with its stream flowing between low hills, *Mazi* (1986) creates a different response because of the aggressive pointed triangle of the yellow shape outlined in black on the lower right, and the ominous stippled grey sky above the low horizon. Kahn knows how to use land—or dreamscapes—to call forth wide differentiations of emotional responses. In *Natah* (1987) and *El Kudeh* (1989), a gigantic black arch occupies the frontal plane. In the former we see an ocean, and in the latter the sands of the desert appear behind the great span. In *Otza II* (1987), the motif of the arch, painted the color of topaz, assumes the appearance of a great rock formation that reaches across a purple field from which a small rocky island seems to emerge. Four black menhirs rise ominously from a dark orange ground contained by a wide black framing enclosure in *Yuna* (1988). In *Rigua*, painted a year later, the viewer seems to be looking down from a cliff upon a rose-colored widespread space at dawn. Small rocks animate the surface of a sea that merges harmoniously with the sky.

After 1990, forms other than landscapes, seascapes and skyscapes are often suggested in Kahn's paintings. A beautiful red flower in front of a floating rock is denoted in *Lyje* (1991), while limbs and curves of the female body are intimated in *Tyhnu* (1991), where the blue and the flesh-colored forms both intermesh and, simultaneously, advance and recede in relation to each other. This reversible relationship between figure and ground stimulates the observer's perceptual illusions. A painting like *Ilica* (1993) can again be seen as a dune landscape metamorphosing into organic anthropomorphic forms. In *Rigu-Saar*, of the same year, a spectre-like purple figure seems to be standing on yellow sand between two green cliffs, while there is a blue lake with a green island below. But this is probably too literal a reading of a mysterious—not a narrative—picture. Paintings like *Luzzan* (1993) and *Ohalim* (1995) are done in organic, muted colors with luminous surfaces and are totally open to free association. The shimmering shape of metallic gold and powdered pewter that appears as the top of the broken ellipse in *Almah II* (1993) does appear like a floating bird with wings outspread, while vibrating volcanic fissures penetrate a fiery red field in *Yshaar* (1994). *Madai* (1995), with its many overlaps, is $2\frac{1}{2}$ inches in thickness and alludes to the appearance of protoplasmic cells; it may very well be based on Kahn's studying electron micrographs of biomorphic images.[11]

A recent painting of great tranquillity and peace is *Ornat* (1995). It once more suggests the waters of the sea, but, as mentioned earlier, there are no specific referents in Kahn's work. His paintings and his sculptures, executed with consummate

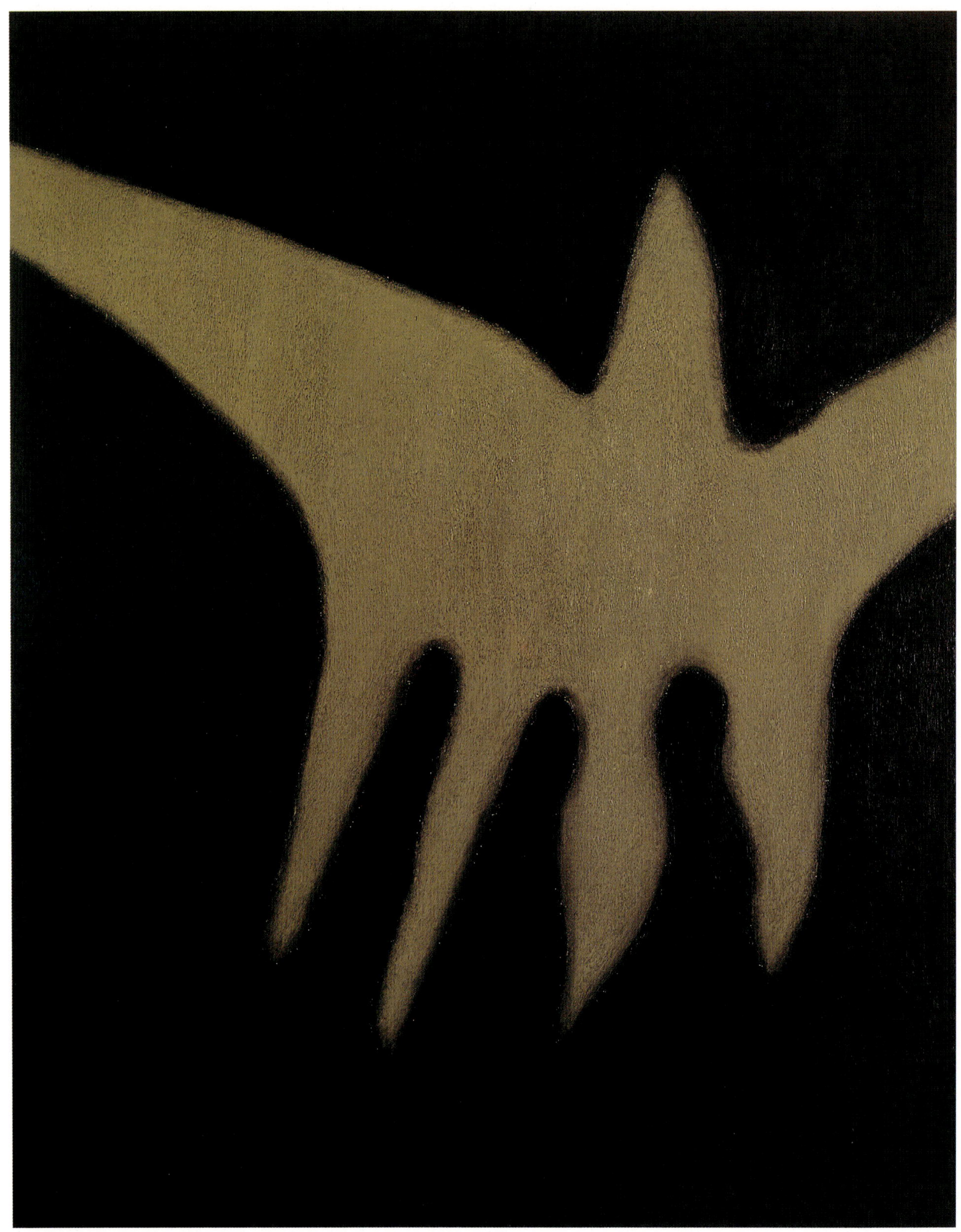

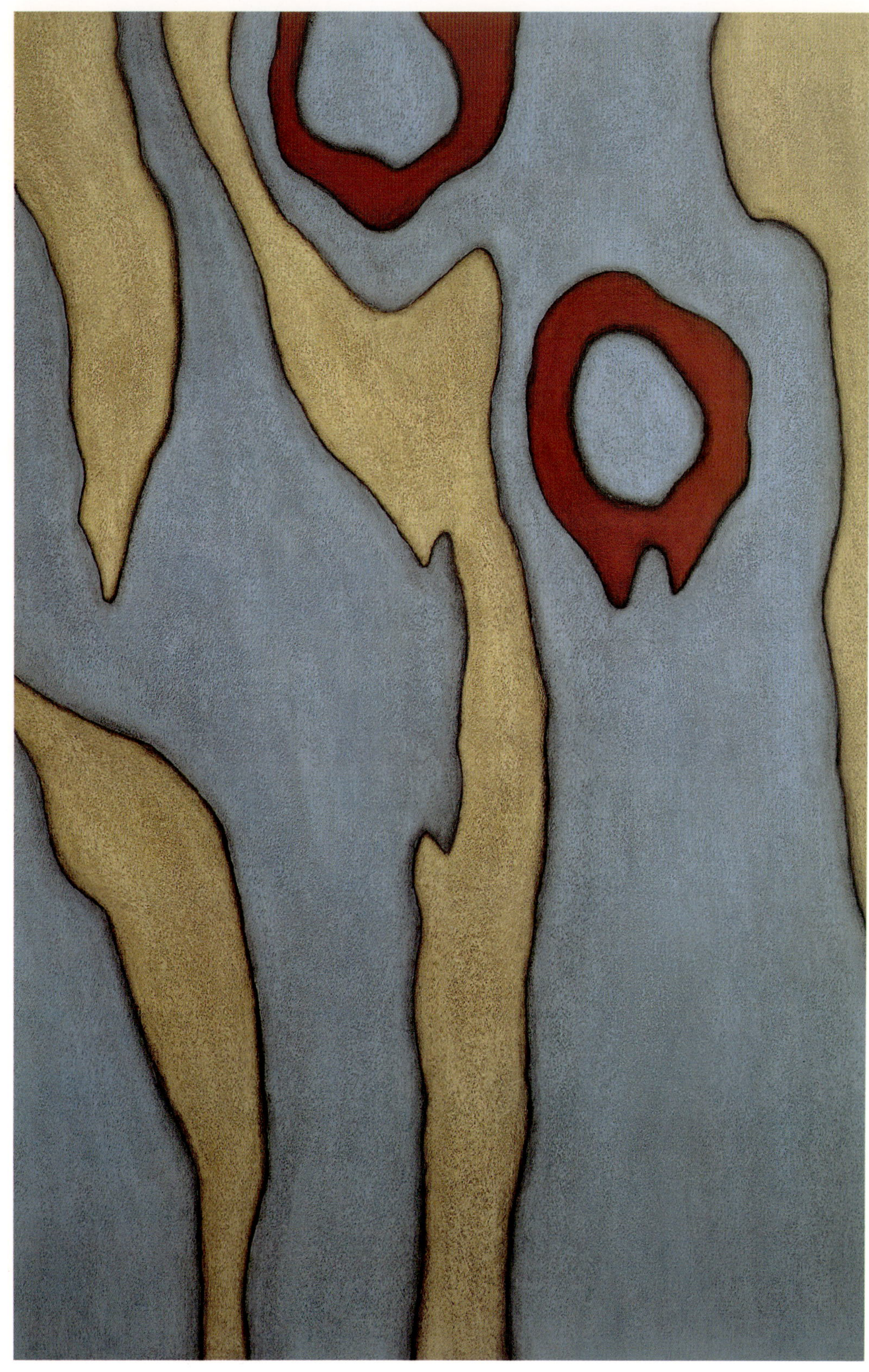

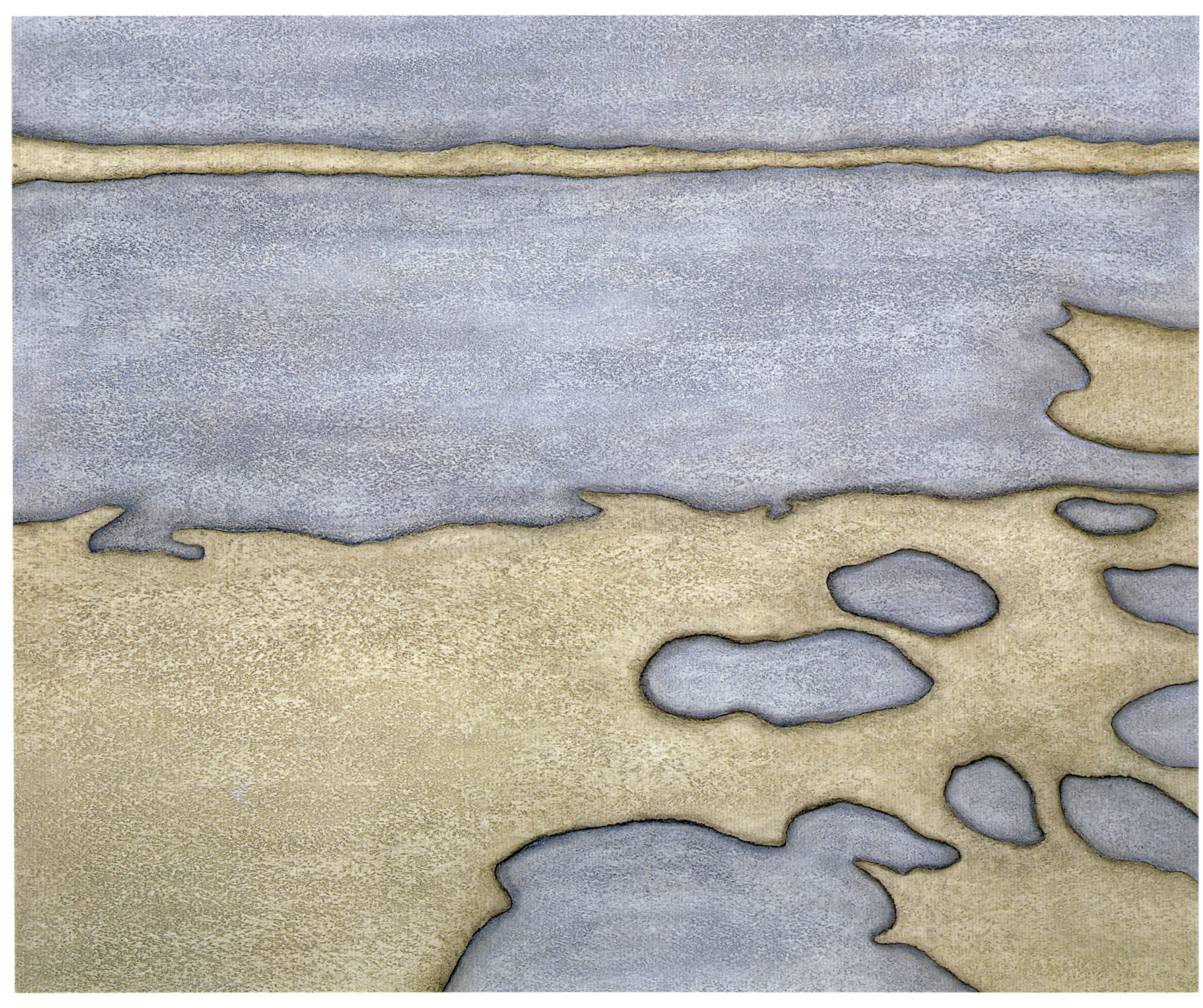

craftsmanship, are animated by a yearning for the transcendent. At a time when the concept of beauty has become anathematized in critical discourse and the perception of the spiritual remains marginalized in the discussions of the art world, Tobi Kahn produces works that combine visual calm with pictorial energy. In their authenticity they affirm art's salutary potential. Not unlike the paintings by the artists mentioned at the beginning of this essay, Tobi Kahn's work fuses observation, memory and making—what Walter Benjamin called "the concrete totality of experience." Kahn's paintings provide a path where the outer world (landscape) and the inner world (creative power) begin to merge.

Nature, it seems, must always clash with Art.
And yet, before we know it, it seems one,
I too have learned: Their enmity is none
Since each compels me, and in equal part...

GOETHE
(tr. by Michael Hamburger)

1. Caspar David Friedrich, Bekenntnisse, K.K. Eberlien, ed. (Leipzig: Klinkhardt & Biermann, 1924), p. 121.

2. Charles Baudelaire, "What is Romanticism," in *The Salon of 1846*. Translated and edited by J. Moyne (London: Phaidon Press, 1965), p. 46.

3. Cf. Barbara Novack, *American Painting of the 19th Century* (New York: Praeger Publishers), chapters 5–7.

4. Marsden Hartley, *Adventures in the Arts* (New York: Boni & Liveright, 1921), p. 30.

5. Tobi Kahn, quoted in Dominique Nahas, *Sacred Spaces* (Syracuse, New York: Everson Museum of Art, 1987), pp. 14–15.

6. Peter Selz, "Alternative Aesthetics: Quests for Spiritual Quintessence," *Arts*, 62, 2 (October 1967).

7. Kahn, "Memo to *Sculpture* Magazine," May 4, 1994.

8. Kahn, "The Memory of Stone: JCC Holocaust Memorial," unpublished paper.

9. Lisa Dennison, *New Horizons in American Art* (New York: Solomon R. Guggenheim Museum, 1985), pp. 13–14.

10. Kahn, in Susan Tumarkin Goodman (curator), *Jewish Themes/Contemporary American Artists II* (New York: The Jewish Museum, 1986), p. 24.

11. The January 1996 issue of *The American Journal of Pathology* (vol. 148, no. 1) has as its cover a painting by Tobi Kahn that seems to be an intriguing parallel to the scientific investigation in cell engineering by the artist's lifelong friend, the scientist Mark Tykocinski.

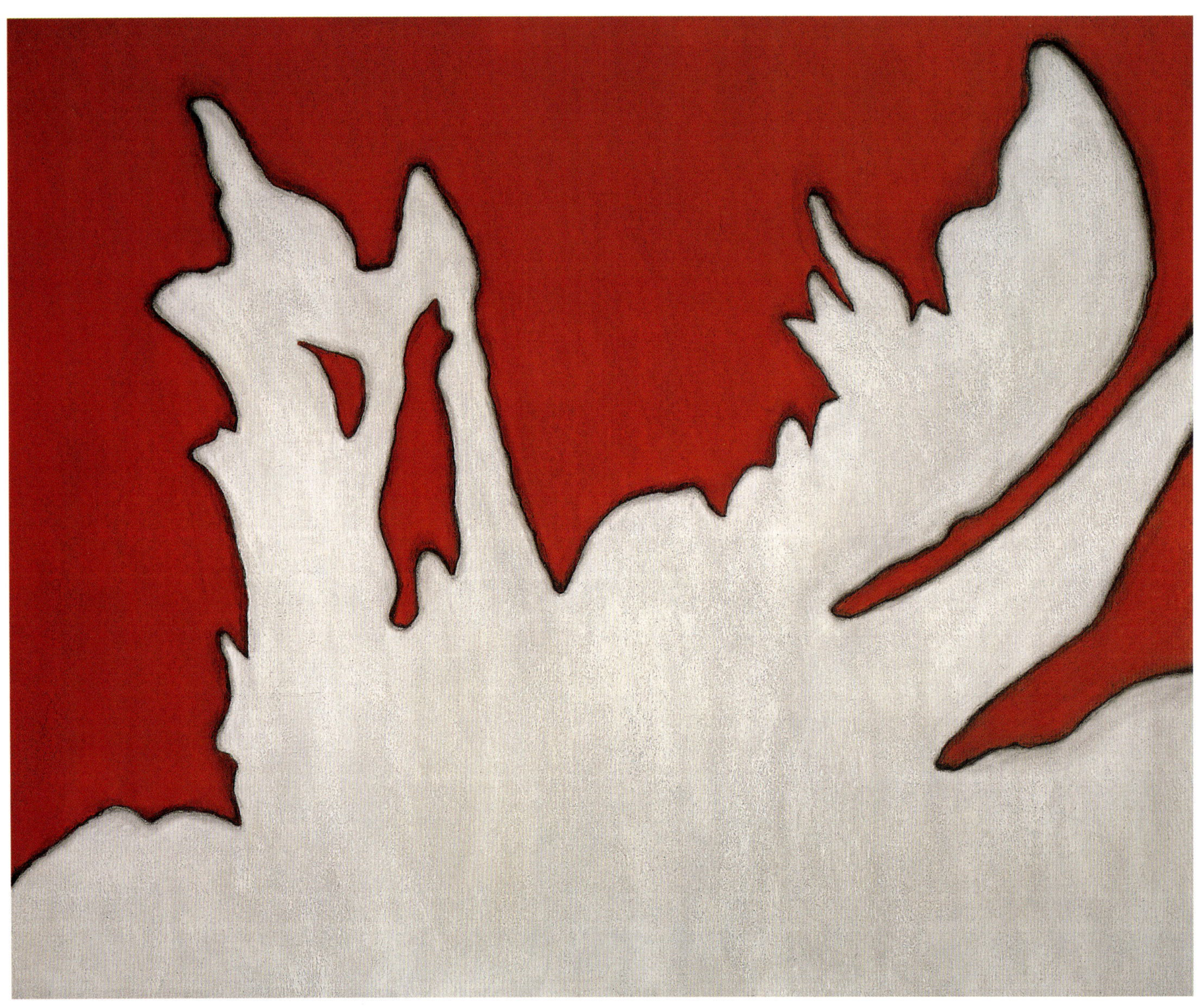

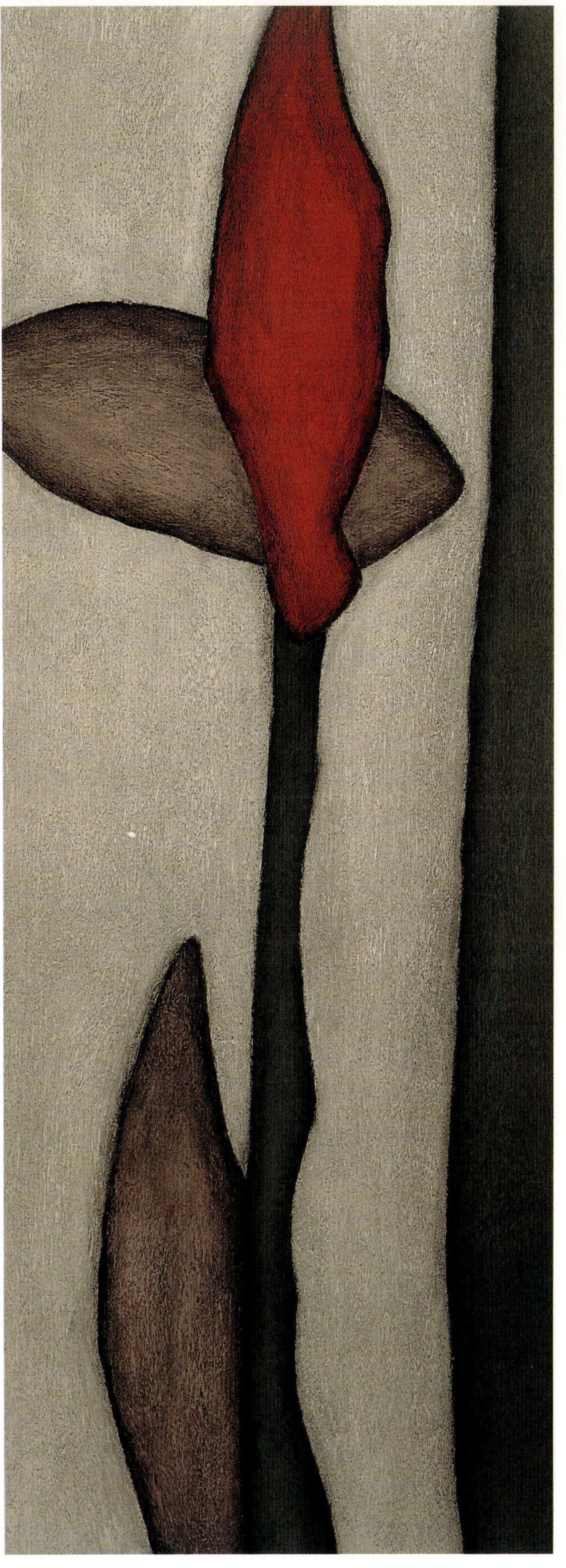

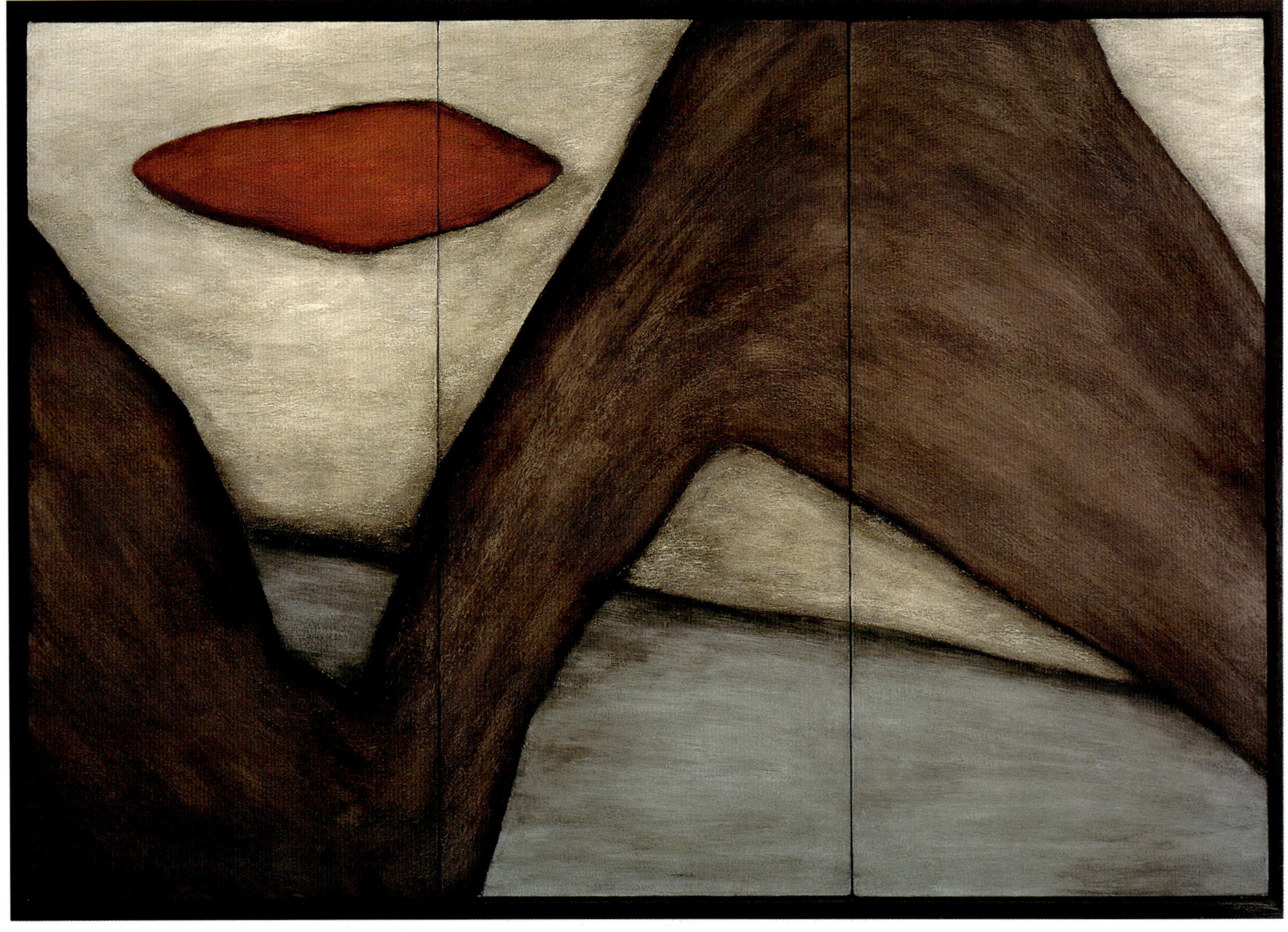

Tobi Kahn's Matter and Memory

DORE ASHTON

One of the dictionary's most engaging definitions of the word abstraction is "the withdrawal from worldly objects." The painter given to abstraction by temperament does withdraw from, turn his eyes from the objects in his world, which nonetheless inform his works. He abstracts *from* them, as so many painters in the modern tradition have insisted. In Kahn's oeuvre, from the beginning, the abstracted elements are always saturated with the sensations of land-sky-sea-cloud-dreamscapes.

Kahn's encounter with matter, whether fluid like water or packed like earth, retreats into memory, much as Henri Bergson had postulated, and is retrieved in the act of painting. His paintings seem to constitute recognitions of sensuous memories as they unaccountably emerge while he works. I would not say that these are dreamscapes, but rather the cumulative evidence of reverie. In reverie, things glide and slide and suggest general rather than specific experiences. Poets have often spoken of the "climate" of reverie, and it is this general climate that permeates Kahn's approach to painting.

Most often Kahn's paintings incite associations with landscape, but landscape transformed by the imagination, as the long romantic tradition demanded. Perhaps the most remarkable avatar was Alexander Cozens, whose treatise *A New Method of Assisting the Invention in Drawing Original Compositions of Landscape* appeared in 1784–86, together with his own illustrations. Cozens's method was based on suggestiveness. If he blotted his ink drawing or crumpled his papers, the blots and crumples set his imagination to work, enabling him to break free from academic conventions. In this startling early enunciation of the principle of free association, Cozens set the conditions for the modern landscape. The role of "invention" took the lead among artists from Delacroix to Seurat, and was tacitly acknowledged in America by Albert Pinkham Ryder, with whom Kahn's works have affinities. Ryder's ability to abstract from his impressions generalized forms and lights is most apparent in his radical simplification of clouds in lunar seascapes. He "invents" the rhymes of sky and sea, sail and cloud, in the poetic manner advocated by his near contemporary, Edgar Allen Poe.

Even in the late 19th century, when artists, like everyone else, were interested in scientific observations concerning perception and representation, it was understood that the artist, after all, was not reproducing facts of nature. The renowned scientist Herman von Helmholtz, writing on the relations of optics to painting in the late 1870s, made clear that "the representation which the painter has to give of the lights and colors of his object, I have described as a translation...." An artist, then, must reveal, not record; must find his own language for his optical experiences.

In the 20th century, the probing of the nature of nature fanned out into many translations, with which an eminently cultured painter such as Kahn is thoroughly familiar. There were the attempts to simplify, to extract the essence of natural forms, apparent in the drawings of Matisse or the paintings of Arthur B. Dove. There were the effusive experiments of using multiple perspectives (drawn of course from the Renaissance traditions), which in the case of Kandinsky, for instance, culminated in his abstractions of 1913. There were translations of natural forms that seemed to be metamorphosing on the plane in a practice that came to be called biomorphism. And there were the attempts to fuse all of painting's means — line, color, space — into the most simple of conditions, a kind of *Ursprache* of painting that ranged from Mondrian's grids to Pollock's arabesques.

If I think of the character of Kahn's work; if, in other words, I am musing about what I have seen, away from the object itself, I always have a feeling of its materiality, its weight. Perhaps his practice of working layer upon layer, attentive to each grain of pigment, colors (literally) my perception. For Kahn's very process, although hidden finally, expresses itself as we look. His shapes, grown from the ground up to almost bas-relief proportions, carry with them the experience of their shaping. And as if to accent our perception of the slow growth of each final surface, Kahn occasionally shadows the final contours of his shapes, so delicately that we can scarcely discern the sources of his light. This, I think, is the "climate" of his work, an almost Wordsworthian recollection in tranquillity. (Which is not to say that Kahn's lyrical imagination is tranquil, nor was Wordsworth's).

There are premonitions in the earlier works in this exhibition. While the allusions are much more obviously to landscape in a conventional definition, they are already once removed from immediate recognition. In *Natah* (1987), there is a clear horizon, although diagonal; a body of water; a sign for a cloud; and a great dark shape, perhaps of a tree, serving as the traditional repoussoir. The light can be called northern, wintry, like the light in late Marsden Hartley Maine landscapes. But two years later, in *El-Kudeh*, the lights are shifting. The great arching shape that straddles the entire picture plane is not so easily named (although to me, this shape and a number of still more curious formations in later paintings suggest the fantastic arches and orifices found in the sandstone walls of Canyon de Chelly). There are ambiguities of light that defy a conventional reading.

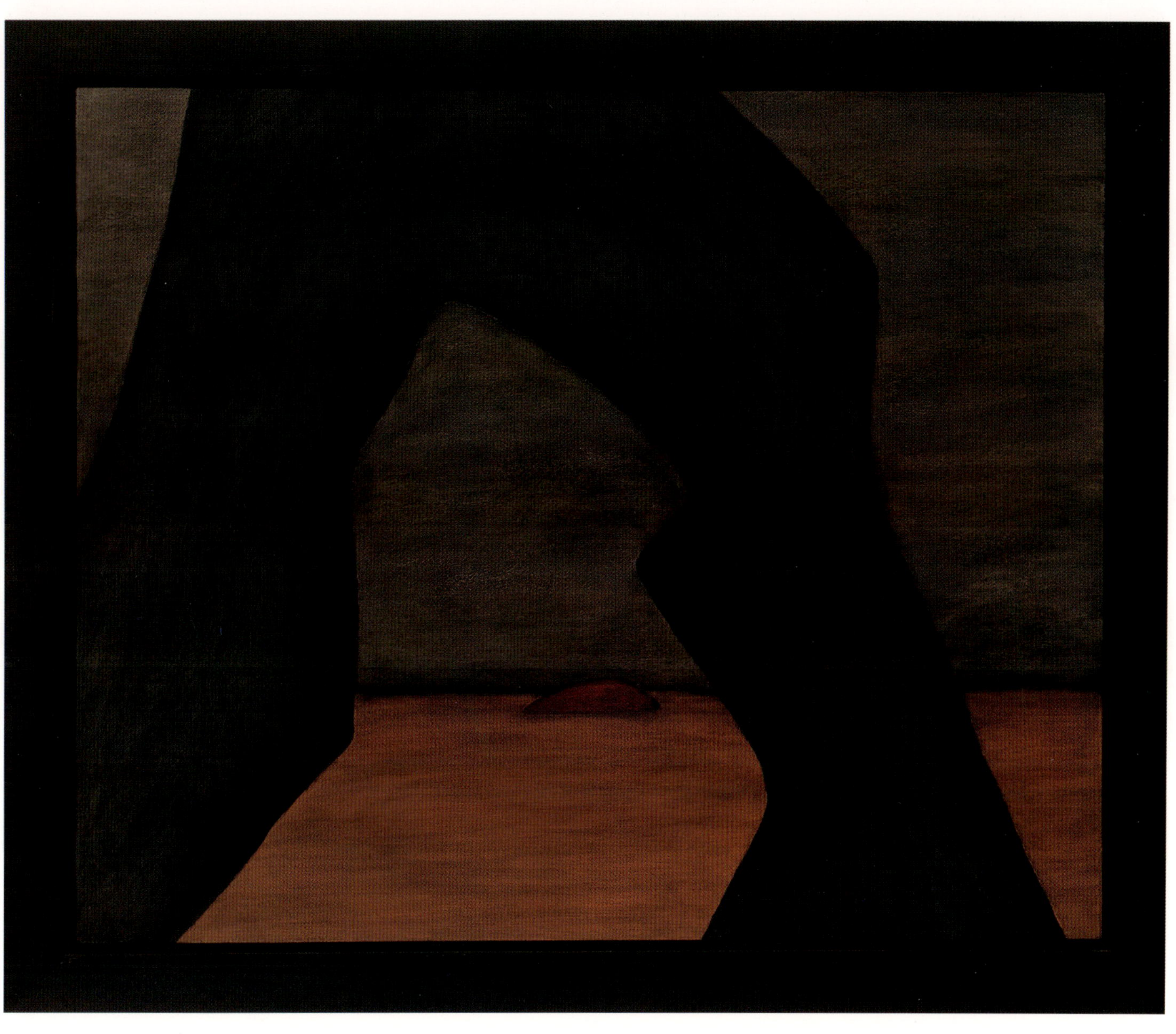

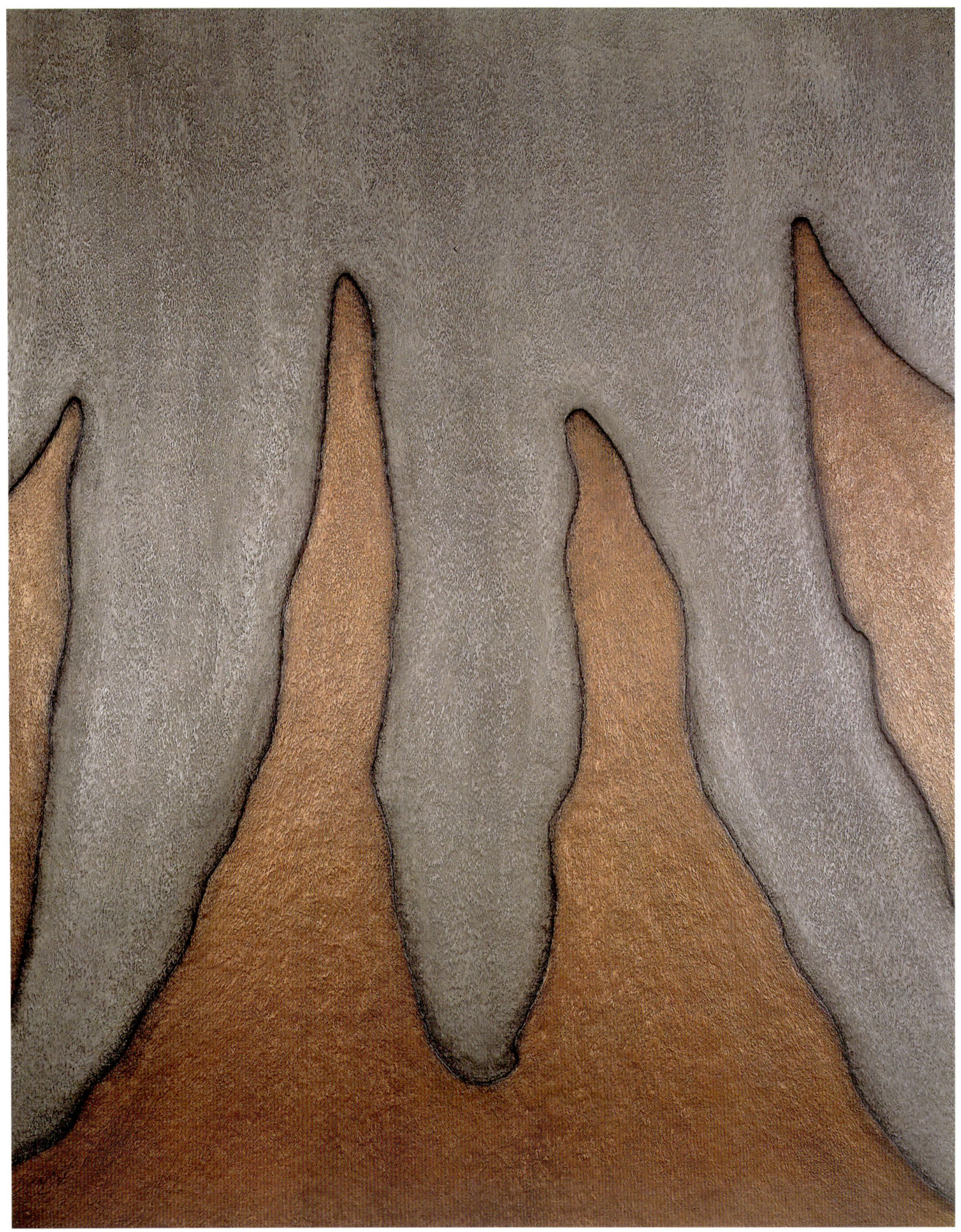

By 1990, Kahn's imaginative allusions to natural form take on almost surrealistic overtones. A vertical composition, such as *Lyje*, might seem plantlike at first glance, but quickly transforms itself into an uneasy conjunction of opposite traits. The strange shape behind the scarlet bloom is more like one of Magritte's levitated stones than it is like a cloud; and the leaf below, similar in tone and surface, might be a stylized mountain or a cleft in the earth, depending on which perspective the viewer assumes.

This matter of perspective: Painters have always been lured by the conundrums implicit in their métier. Long before there were aircraft, artists experimented with the bird's-eye view, sometimes combining a looking down with a looking up on a single canvas. For a modern painter this is a natural way to consider the picture plane, but there is still a degree of visual uneasiness when groundlines vanish. It is this spatial ambiguity that provides the tension in several of Kahn's recent paintings. Despite the simplicity of composition—two tones and a few finger-like shapes—of *Ohalim*, there is a figure-ground challenge. Associations shift. The silvery overtones suggest water, but then, if read alternately, the shapes suggest roots. Earthen tones, like grains of sand, also shift in and out of focus, as they do in *Madai*, where the flow of deep blue might suggest water, but then, what are those deep red shapes floating upward?

Kahn's versatility in building tones to create a climate of thought—that is to say, a mode of translation—is evident in a work such as *Ornat*. Here, everything is irradiated by a secret light whose source is just beneath the surface. Mist, fog, opalescent undertones unify, generalize the experience. But once the apparent horizon line is registered, the system of relief seems reversible, and in the drawing (emphasized by shaded contour lines) shapes begin to transform themselves. Although Kahn is always mindful of a foreground, middle ground and background as he works, these conventional ways of considering the picture plan give way to inventions that put everything in question, including the point of view of the spectator. It is in this constant convertibility that the apparent simplicity of Kahn's vision is belied.

Kahn, then, describes the edges of waking experience, in much the way he delicately shades the edges of his ambiguous forms. There can be no separating of matter and memory.

Survival Rites

M I C H A E L   B R E N S O N

Tobi Kahn made *Moad* in 1982, five years after he found in the construction of polychrome objects an essential complement to the slow-moving, dream-like fusions in his paintings. The work is steeped in European modernism and Old World culture. Its architectural shape evokes the Russian Jewish villages painted by Marc Chagall in which every oddly proportioned dwelling is alive with memory. It also suggests the steep angles and eccentric perspectives of 17th- and 18th-century buildings in German Expressionist painting and film, which seem bent and twisted by the pressures of modern life. And like some of the architectural fantasies of the Surrealists, it suggests a place that has trapped inside its windowless, doorless interior a personal narrative longing to be released.

But *Moad* is also a figure that is profoundly uprooted, suspended in a moment so absolute that all thoughts of past and future seem to have vanished. Its peculiar proportions, wedge-shaped roof and immobile dark legs suggest an awkwardness that is less a response to a particular situation than a permanent condition. As a figure, this sculpture, even with its confident uprightness, is an image of outsiderness and alienation. The material is masonite, cut into six pieces, joined and then coated, first with brown oil paint, then with white paint laid on with a palette knife, and finally with a black wash. Because of its thinness and smoothness, the painted surface seems like naked skin, which reinforces the sense of an anxious body with nowhere to hide. The sculpture is hollow, which reinforces the sense of vulnerability. *Moad* is self-contained yet defenseless, protected yet unprotectable, secretive yet exposed. As a building, it suggests place. As a figure, it suggests exile. It is both a repository of collective memory and a personal predicament.

Moad underlines some of the essential characteristics of Kahn's sculpture. It is extremely accessible, in part because its surface is so tactile, but there seems to be an invisible wall between us and it. It seems excruciatingly self-conscious in its wariness and in its regard for the way it is seen, but it is also beyond self-consciousness in its almost confessional openness. It suggests childlike delight and trust through the toy-like quality of its building-block shape and the artist's total absorption in the process of its creation, but in its bottomless anxiety and doubt it suggests an adult struggling constantly with the weight of history.

One of the clearest signs of Kahn's sculptural sensibility is his feeling for scale. *Moad* is 46¾ inches tall, 9¾ inches wide and 8¼ inches thick, but its experiential size seems indeterminate. Although the image is essentially a single block, the interpenetration of its diverse parts—that is to say, the concentration of distinct and often conflicting references and feelings within it—communicates a sense of psychological movement so intense that the skin and shape of the object seem barely able to contain it. *Moad* is a seamless image that argues against the possibility of an integrated self or a unified whole. The sense that the multiple parts within this elegantly economical form will never quite fit together gives *Moad* its discomforting edge.

In situating *Moad* in the recent history of art, think of the New Image artists, who entered the spotlight when Kahn was in art school. Nicholas Africano and Susan Rothenberg painted figures of psychological disruption and subjected them to the pressures of uncharted, if not unchartable, space. Joel Shapiro made sculptures of great psychological intensity in which functional objects like chairs occupied proportionately vast spaces that offered neither community nor solace. Keep in mind, as well, Louise Bourgeois, whose "Femmes-Maisons" may be the most important ancestors of sculptures after 1960 that are both figure and architecture. Bourgeois, Shapiro, Rothenberg and Africano are all dependent to some degree on Alberto Giacometti, whose emaciated, endangered postwar figures asserted with irrefutable eloquence the imaginative potential of sculptural scale.

The presence of the New Image artists and of Giacometti is still important but considerably less evident in the shrines that Kahn began making in 1977 and that constitute his primary sculptural output between 1982 and 1988. These ceremonial theaters, almost all of them less than two feet tall, are at first glance radically different from *Moad*. For one thing, the architecture is less Old World European than Classical. Its rectangular structures bring to mind Greek and Roman temples; some have architectural details that suggest religious monuments of Egypt and Babylon. Like *Moad*, none have windows or doors, but all have roofs and walls and an inner chamber that is visible through an open entrance. Their lines are hard and clean, their proportions familiar. In contrast with *Moad*, the shrines are defined by architecture that appears to carry little or no psychological meaning.

In the shrines, figure and architecture seem distinct. The male or female form, rarely more than a few inches tall, exists alone inside the structure, accessible to the point where viewers seem almost encouraged to reach in and touch it. The figures are created from scrap wood Kahn finds in the streets, takes back to his studio, paints white so that the grain and texture will not affect his perception of its formal identity, and then lives with and carves until the discard dictates to him the site he will

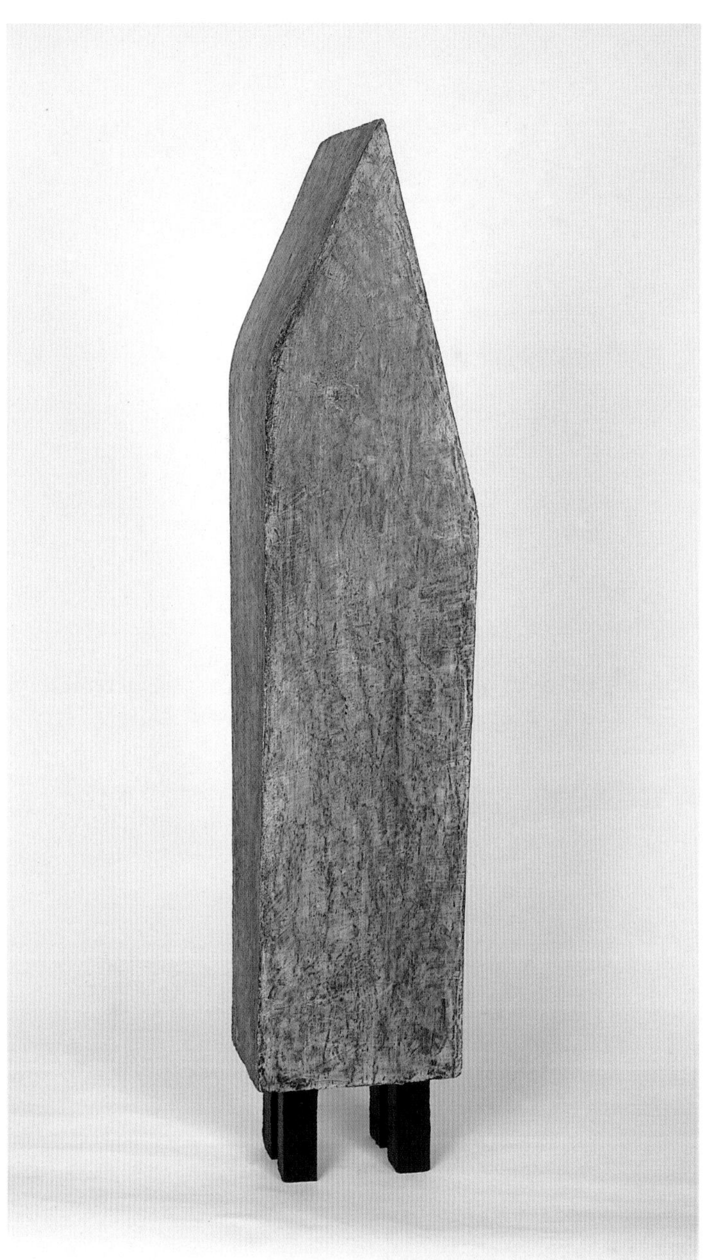

build for it. These religious settings are made of wood, often pine, that Kahn buys. He paints and sometimes washes it with acrylic, which thickens the surfaces and makes his ritual spaces seem that much more venerable and timeless.

Far more than sculptures like *Moad*, the shrines have a performative dimension. The figures may be stretching, or dancing, or engaged in some other physical act. The way they are engaged, even without arms, hands or head, is always unself-conscious. Sometimes it is ecstatic. In part because the torsos are naked, their actions, as well as their natures, can seem pagan. All the figures feel free to be what they are and to throw themselves into their trance-like rituals, which makes physical abandon seem indispensable to the religious act.

But for all the clarity and openness of the shrines, there is something odd, disconcerting, even forbidden about them. The entranceways may be open, but they all seem like thresholds that cannot be crossed. This sense of an invisible barrier can be explained by the stern, frontal architecture and by the cool, often dark colors with which every inch of it, inside as well as out, is painted, as well as by the overhang projecting forward from some of the structures. All of this holds the viewer back and brings into the work the weight of the punitive and the irrational. In part because of the authority of this threshold, the rituals we witness inside the shrines seem to belong to a world we can observe and meditate on but not enter.

The impact of these works depends upon a relationship between figure and architecture every bit as complex as the one in *Moad*. These two components of the shrines are indeed very different, yet in crucial ways the differences break down. The figures are clearly fragments. Just as important, they seem to have always been that way: they may never have been whole. The architecture is fragmented as well, but it does seem to have once been part of a temple, mausoleum, or home. The solitary, uprooted figures depend for protection on a ritual space that is itself solitary and uprooted, broken off from a totality that is no longer visible or even imaginable. The figures are nomadic. But so is the architecture. The shrines are as much emblems of exile as *Moad*. Figure and architecture are very different, yet they are like allies or partners; sometimes like mother and son, or mother and daughter, or lovers. They have been shaped by the same trauma, the same rupture, the same will, the same history.

In the shrines, as in *Moad*, there is a profound sense of misfittedness. While the figures seem to belong to spaces that were especially made for them, while it seems they and only they could rightfully occupy them, the spaces always seem a little bit wrong for them. They are too big or too small for the bodies and for the feelings of loss and desire that exist with such intensity within them. So while there is a profound sense of connectedness in the shrines, there is also a sense of irrevocable disunity. The figures belong to the spaces and the spaces belong to the figures but they do not quite fit together, and both seem forsaken by a world that does not care if they live or die.

All of Kahn's sculptures are on one level about survival. They are post-Holocaust works by a first-generation American whose observant Jewish parents experienced Nazism first-hand. In his shrines, Kahn does not articulate the experience of exile, as he did in *Moad*, although he makes its psychological cost clear. Instead he transforms it into a condition of possibility. On their own, Kahn's figures and architecture and architectural figures not only endure but point toward a spiritual realm in which outsiderness, doubt and conflict will be not stamps of dishonor but marks of the chosen. And toward an aesthetic realm in which an experience of brokenness and fragmentation will be indispensable to an encounter so intense and distinct that it will seem whole.

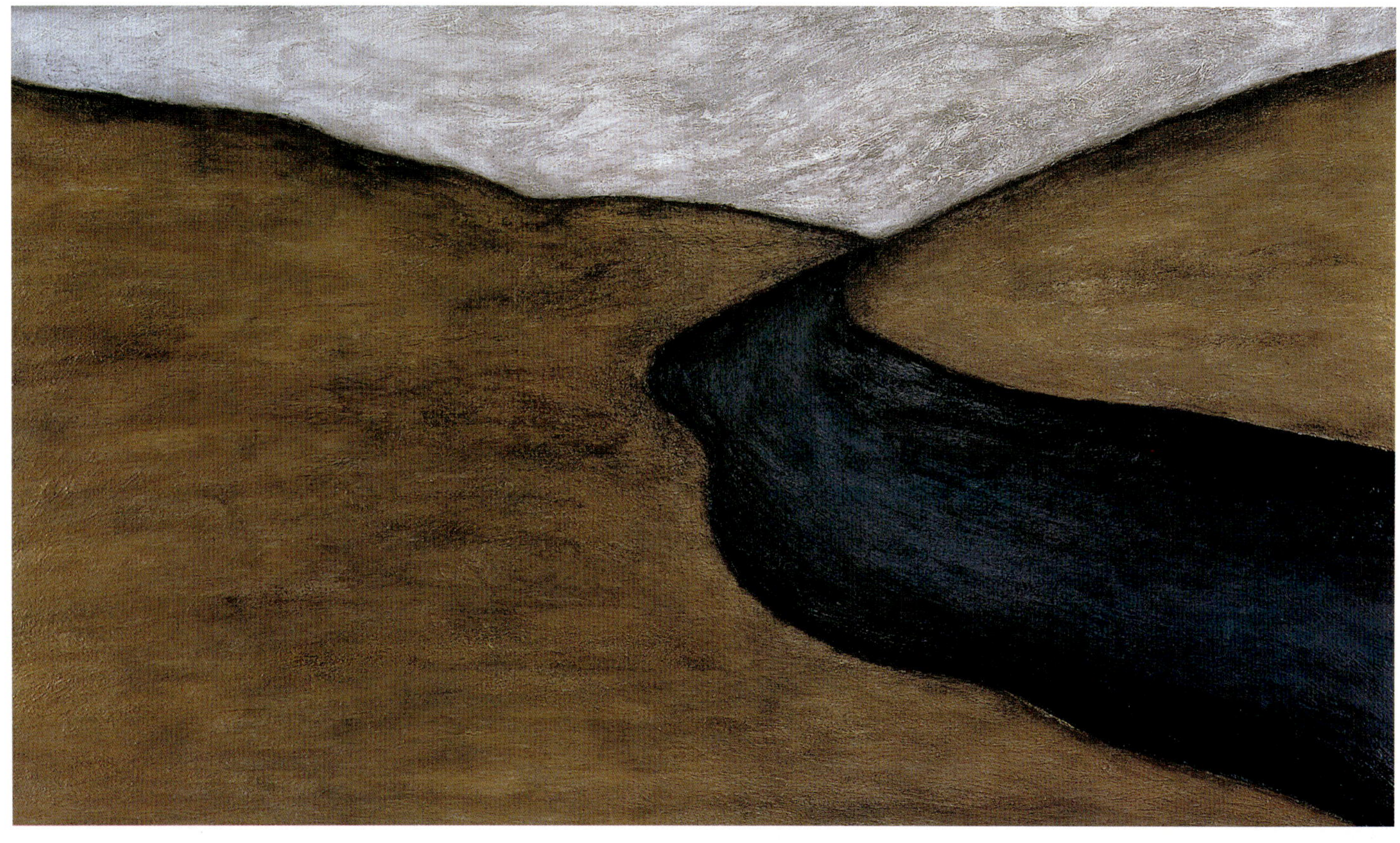

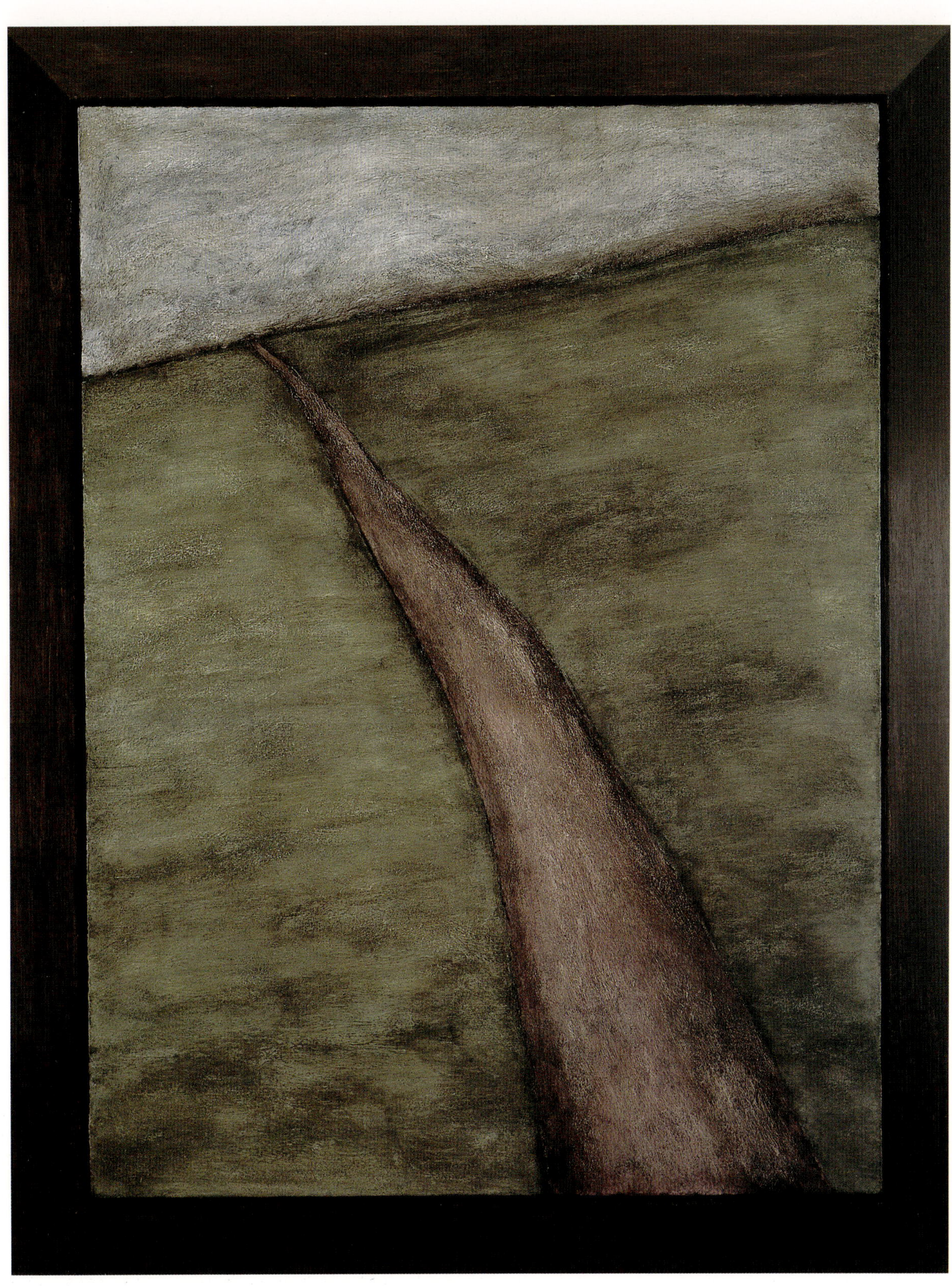

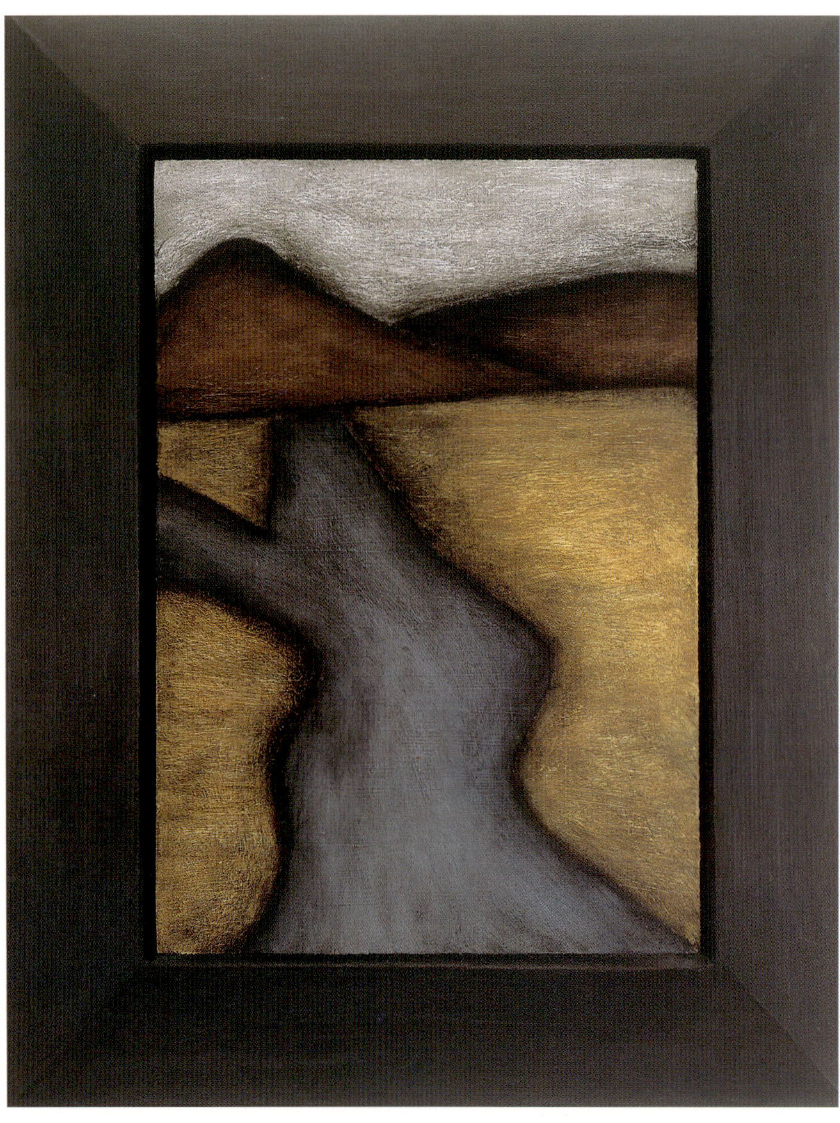

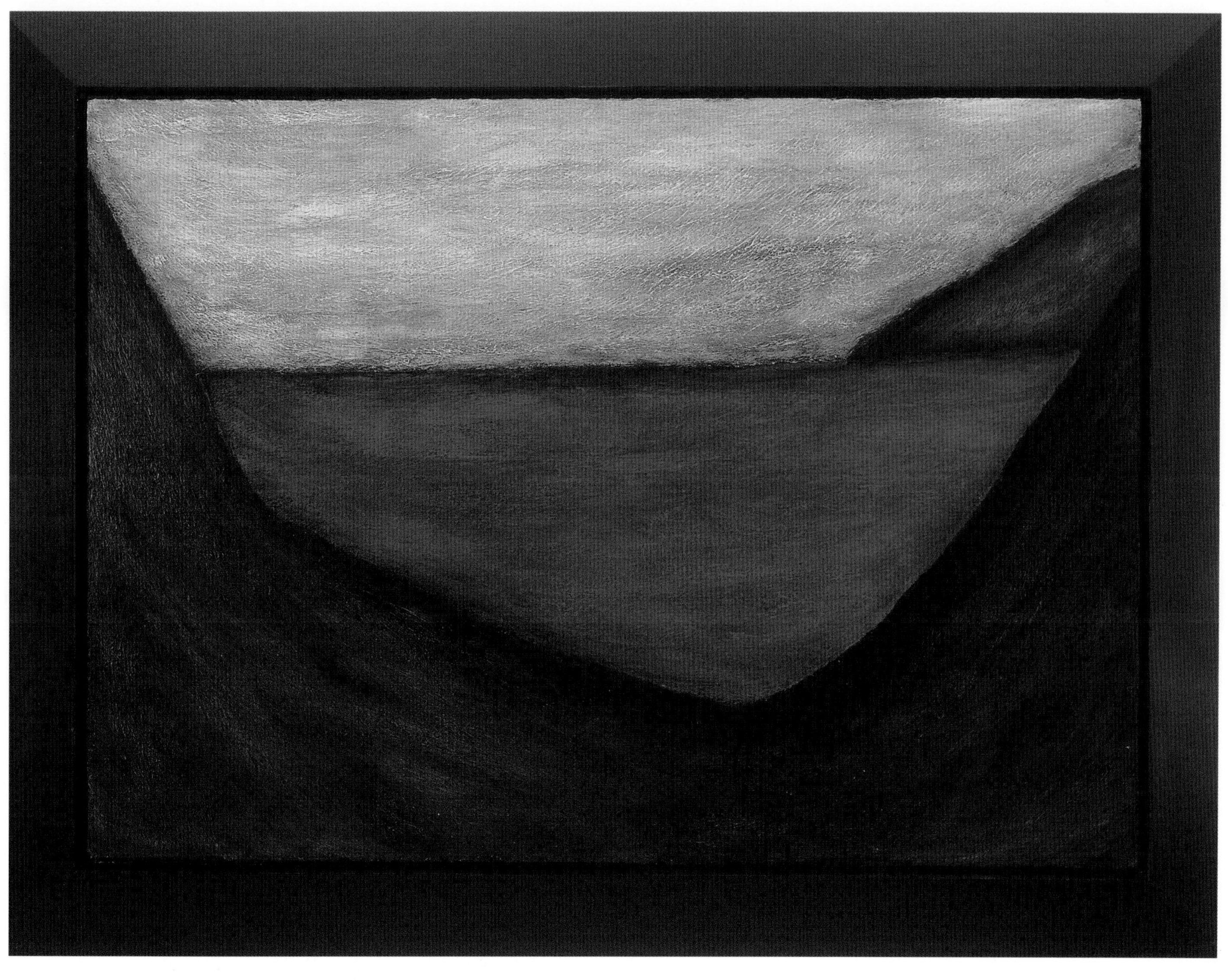

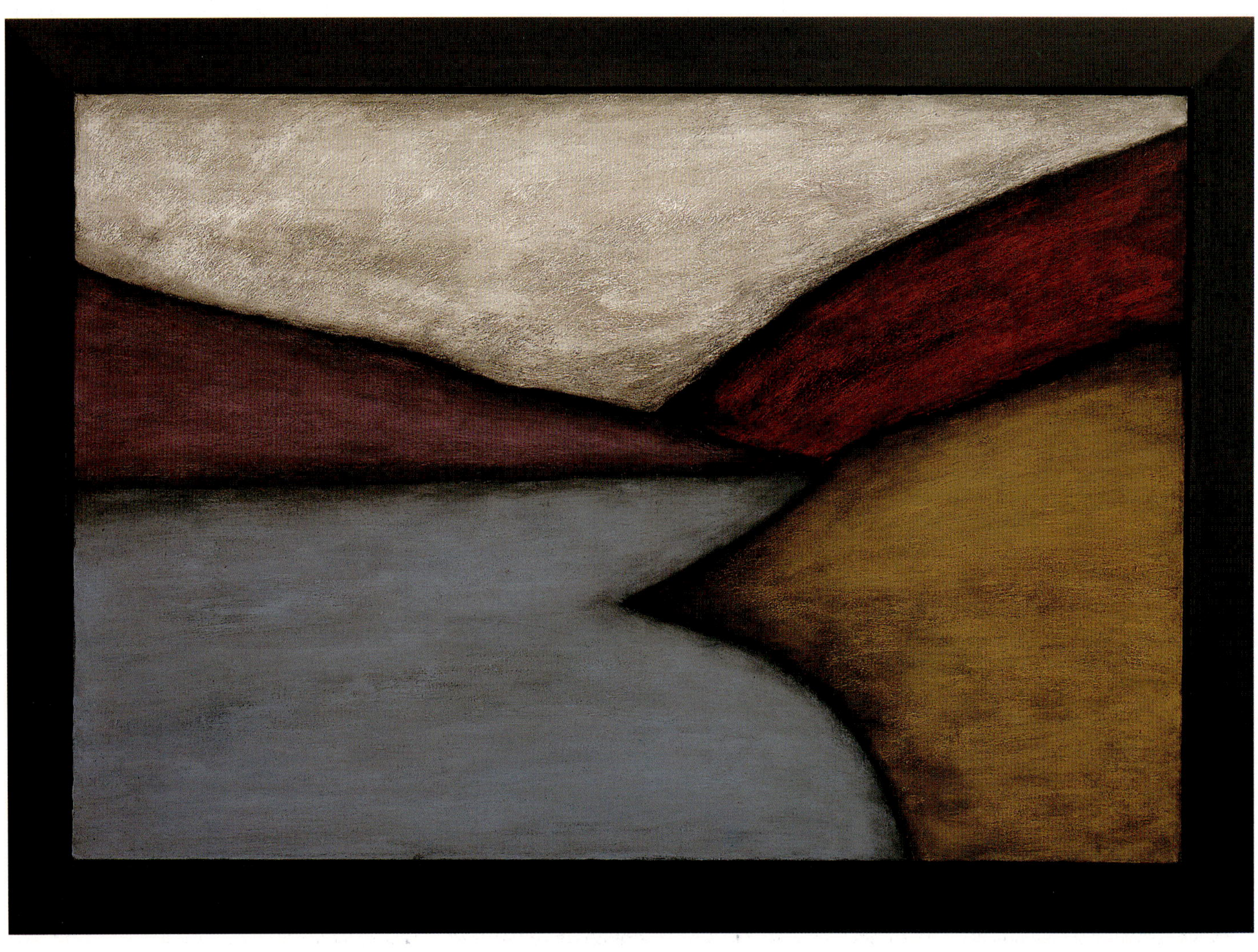

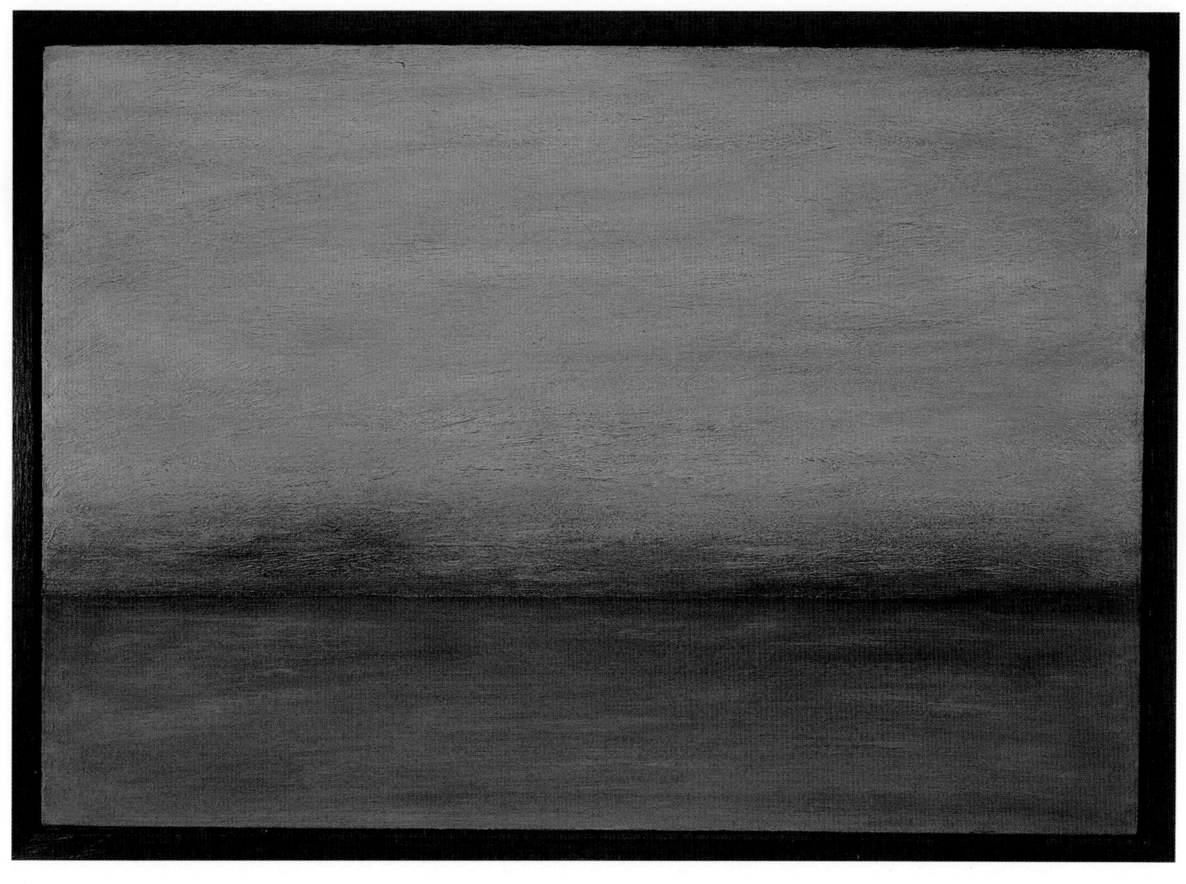

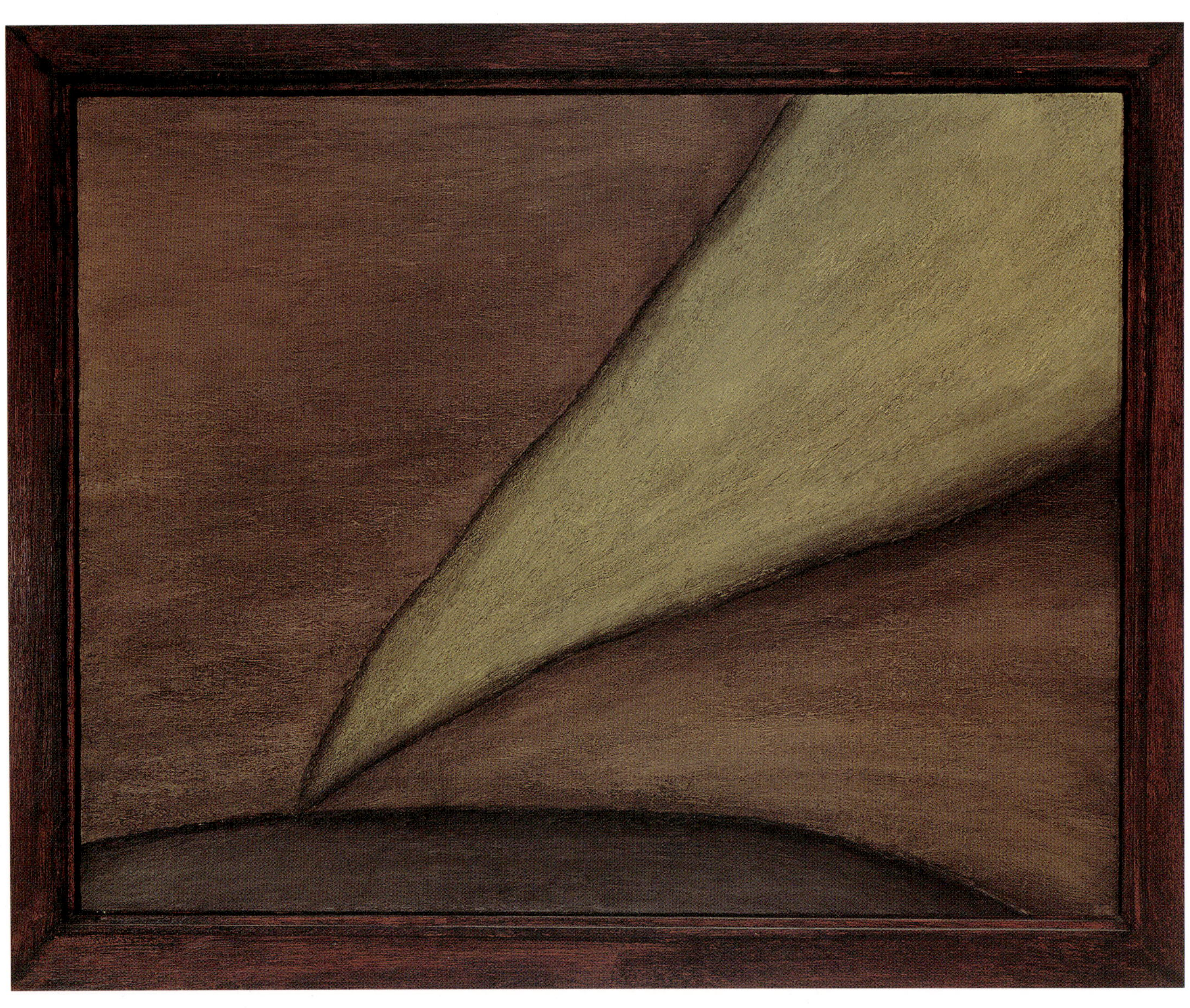

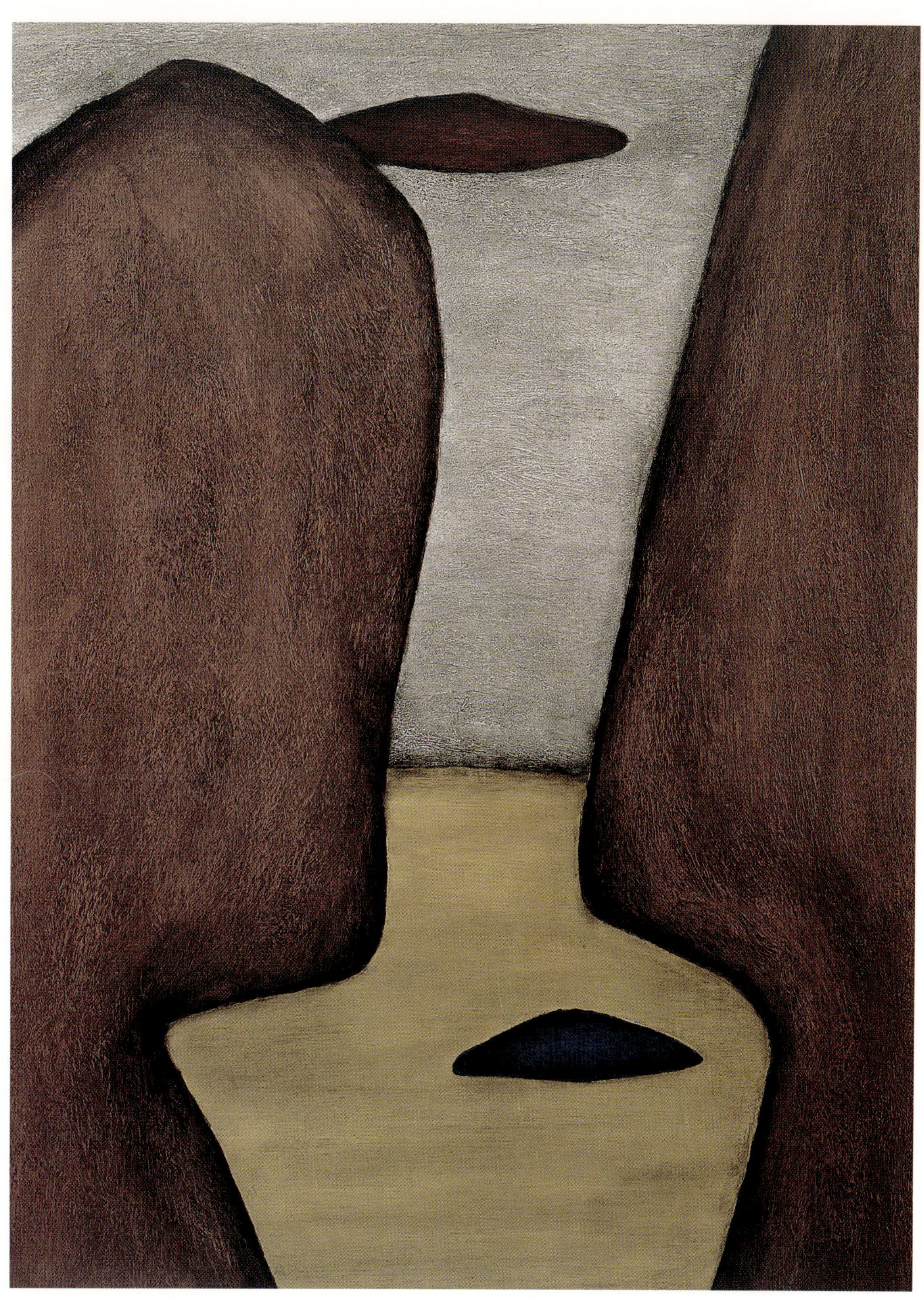

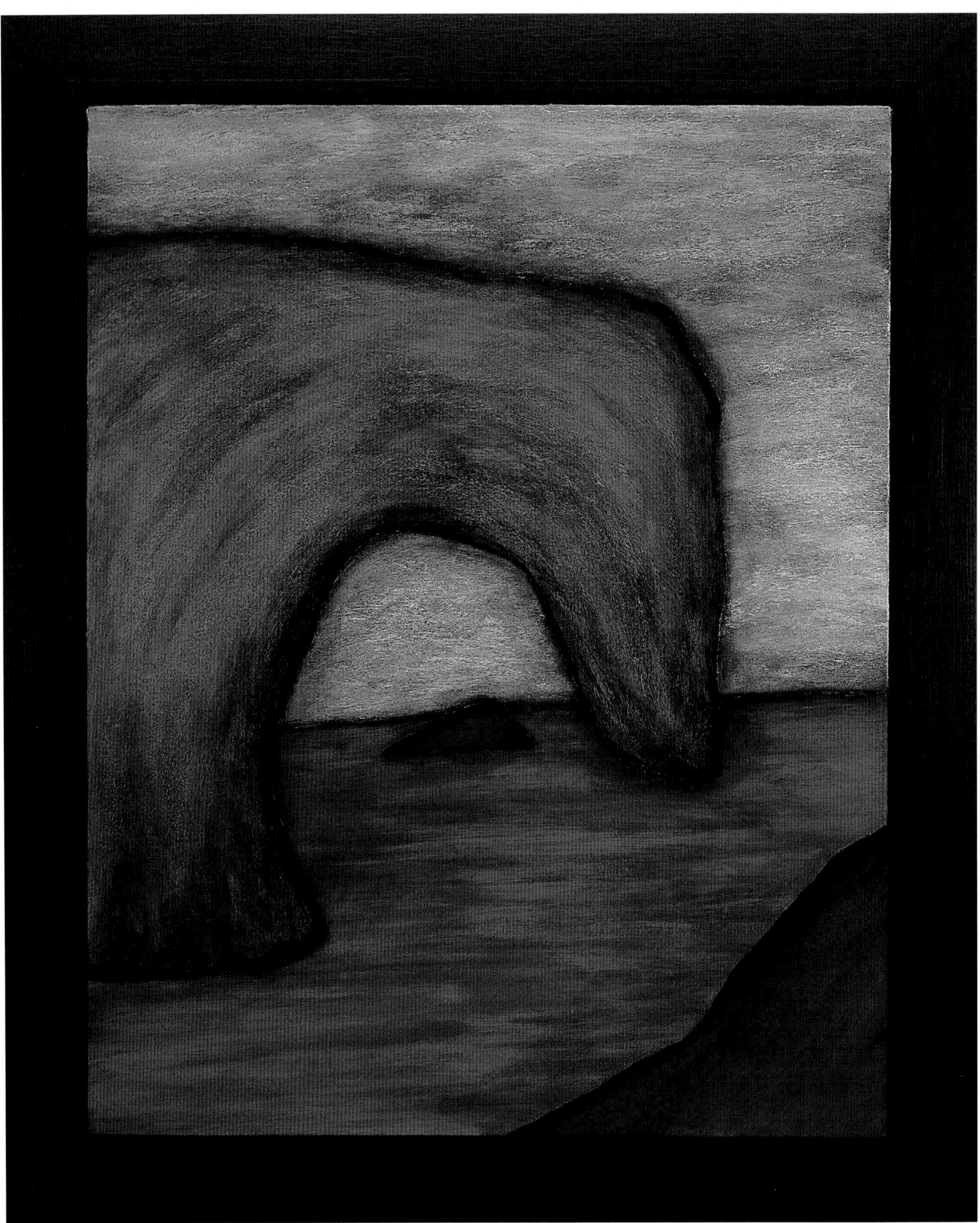

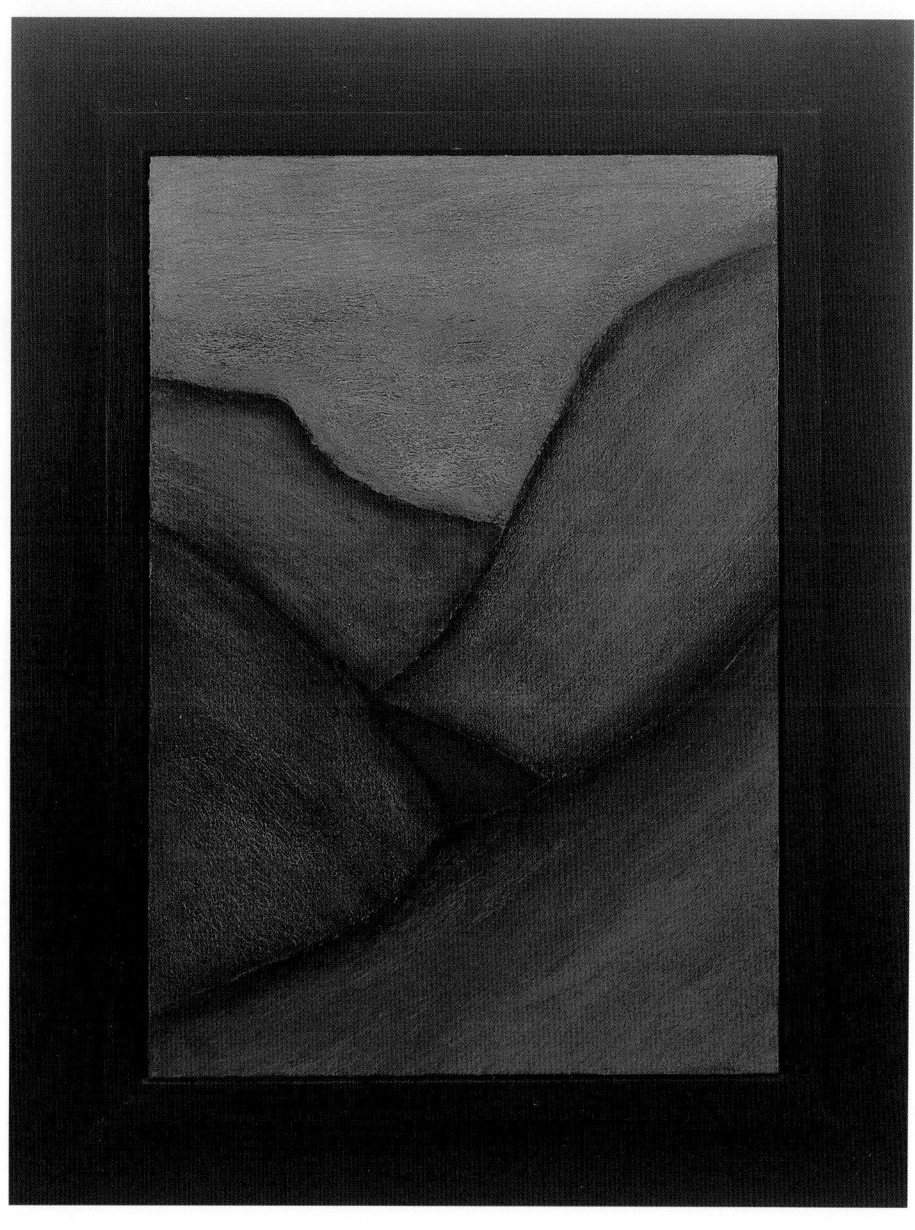

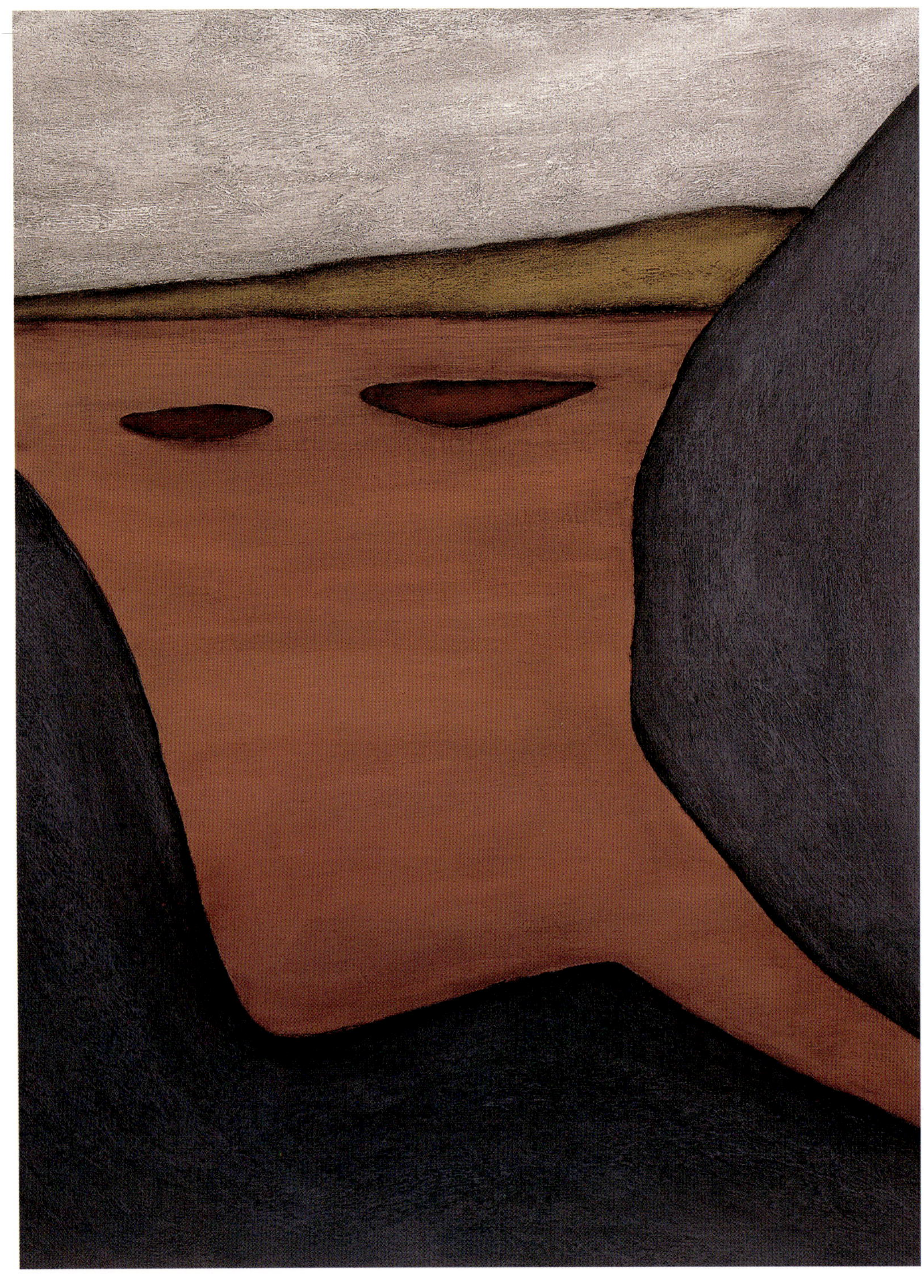

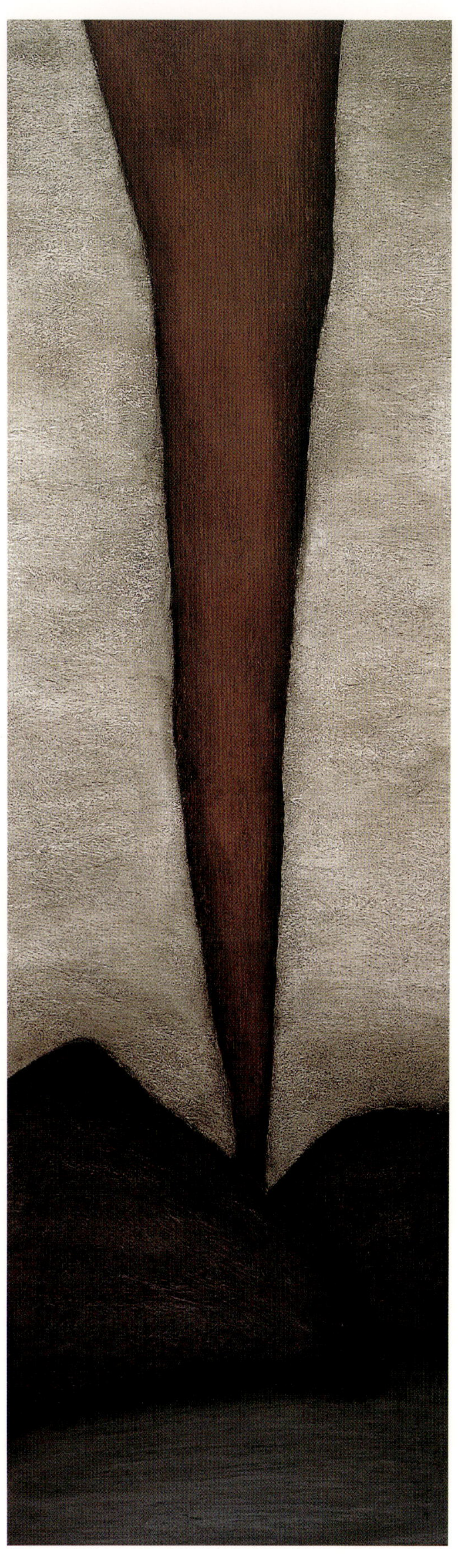

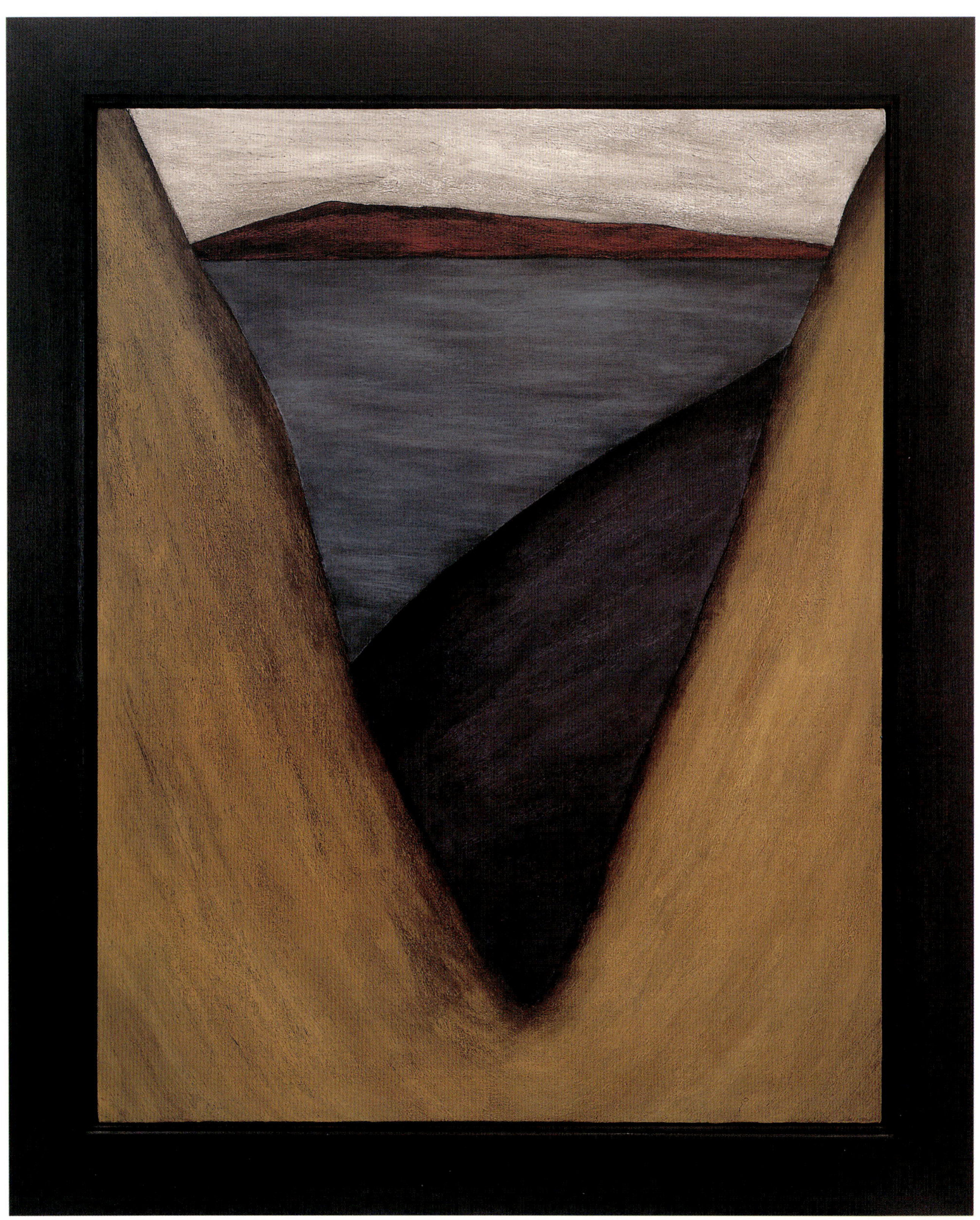

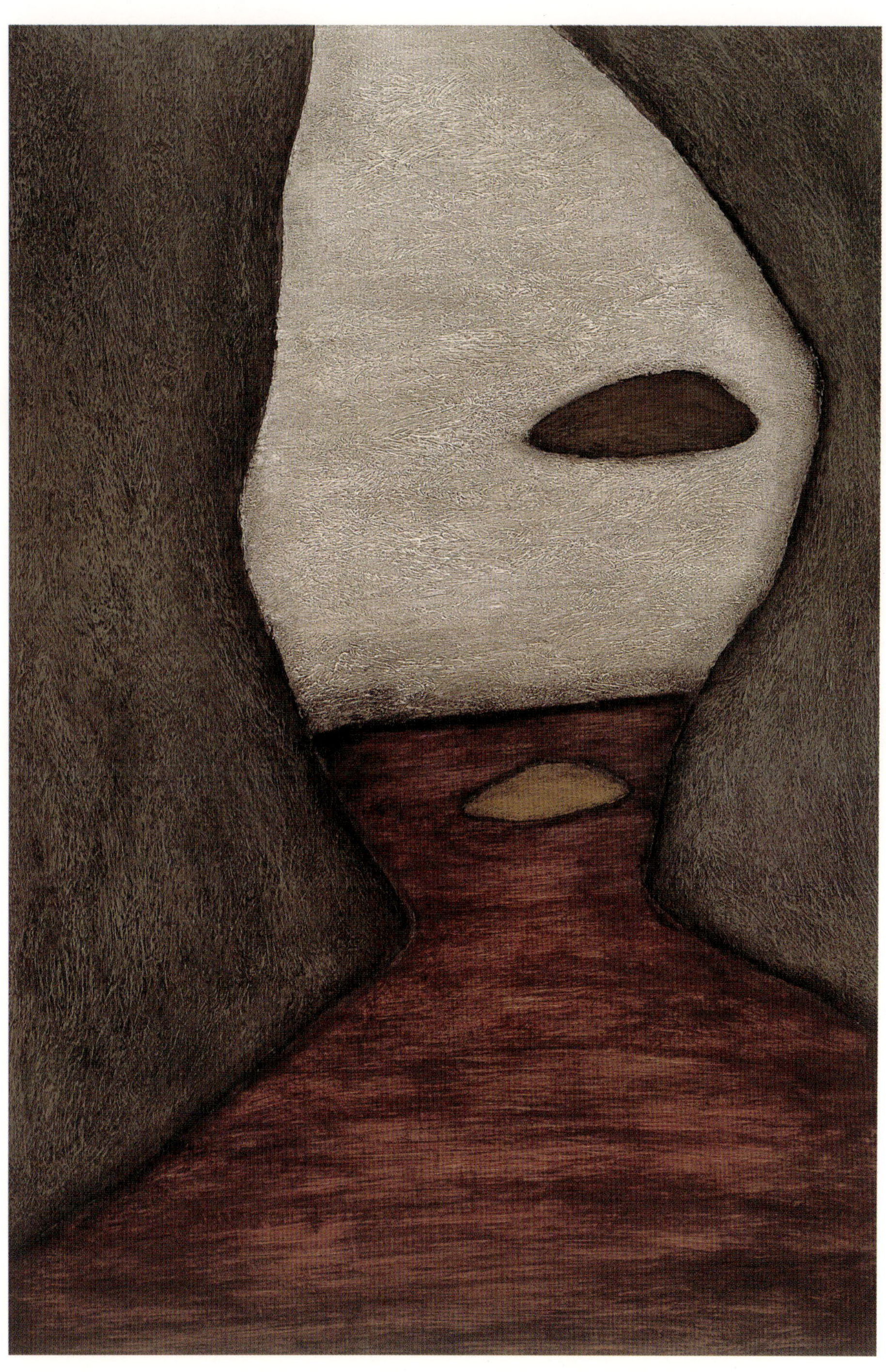

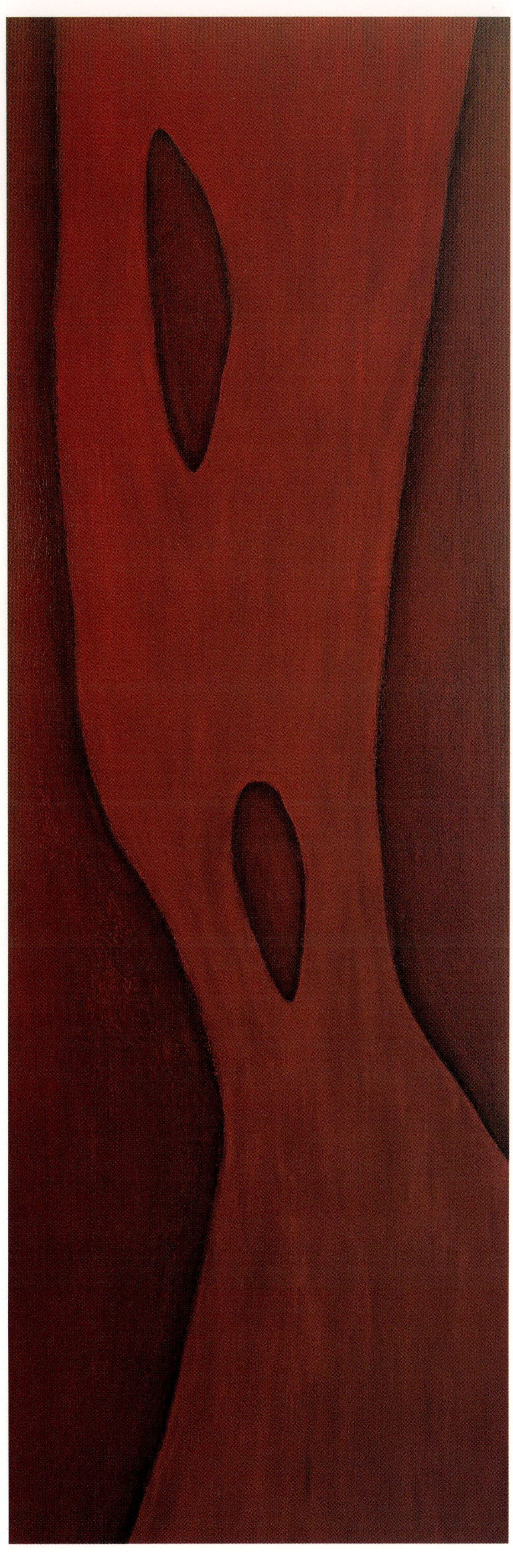

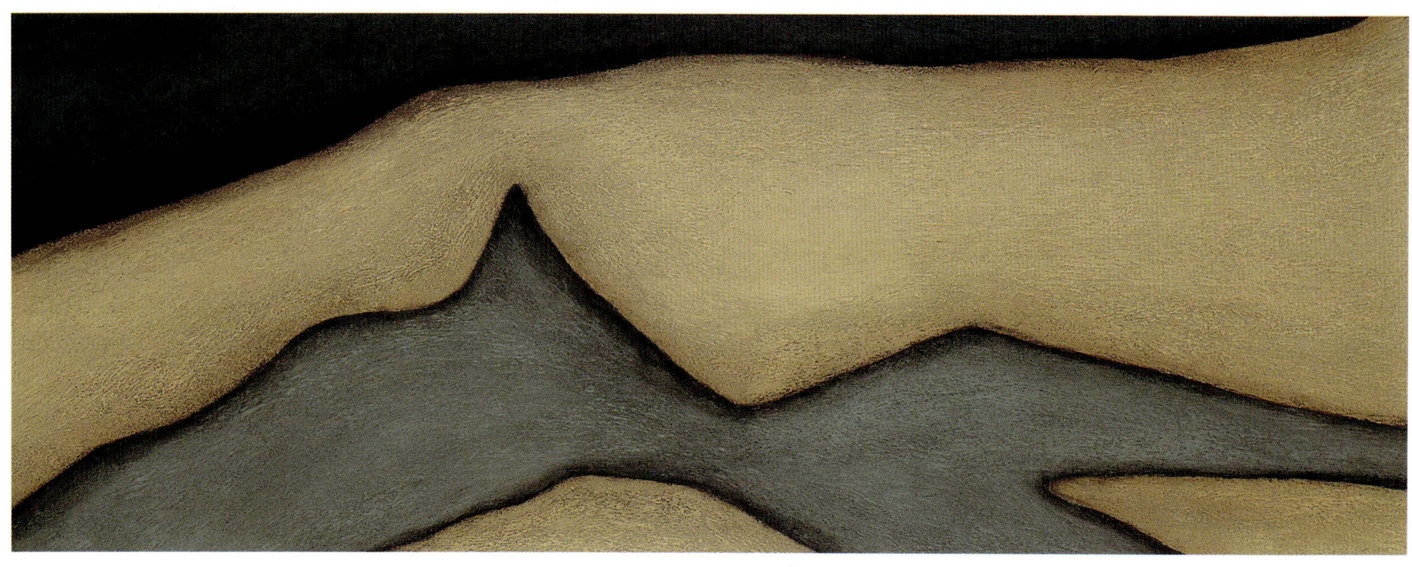

I X Q U A | 1992 *cat. 24*

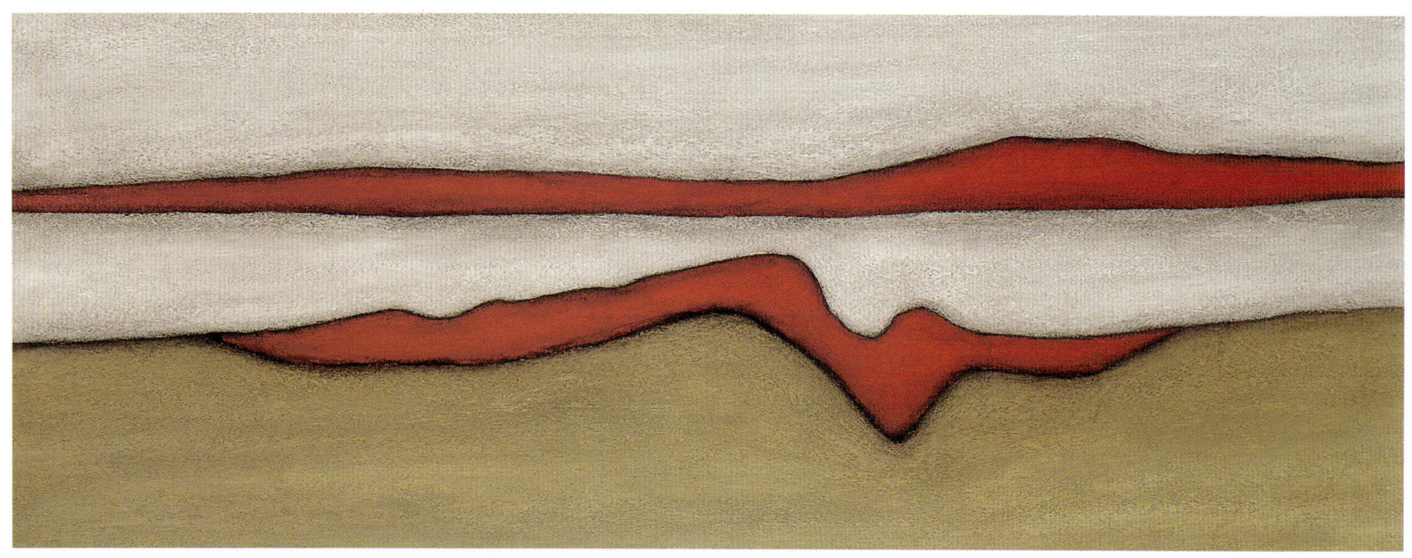

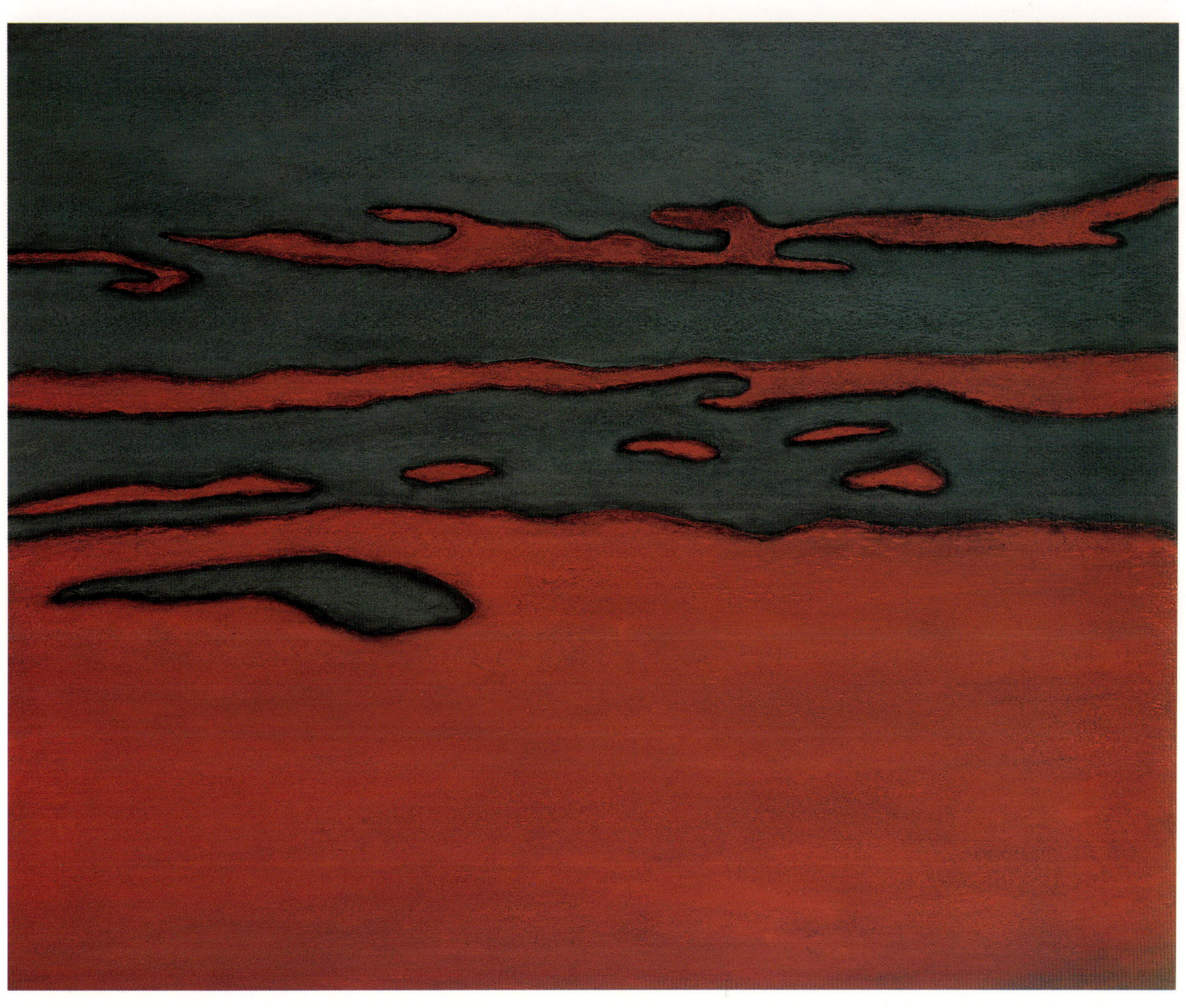

ILICA | 1993 *cat. 25*

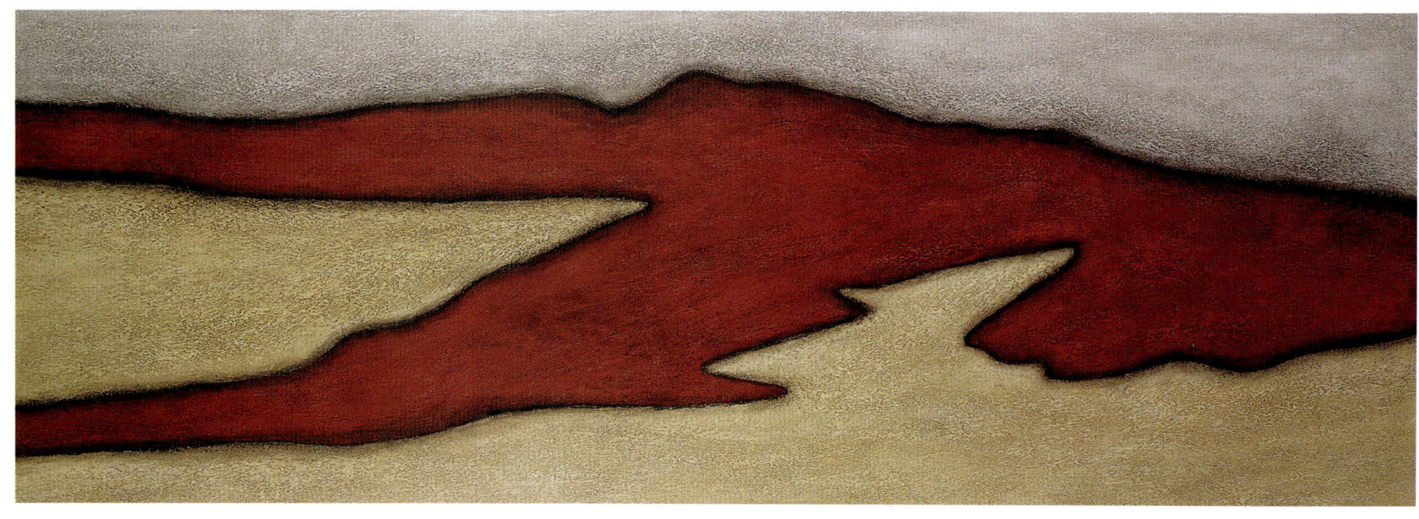

ORRAH | 1993 *cat. 27*

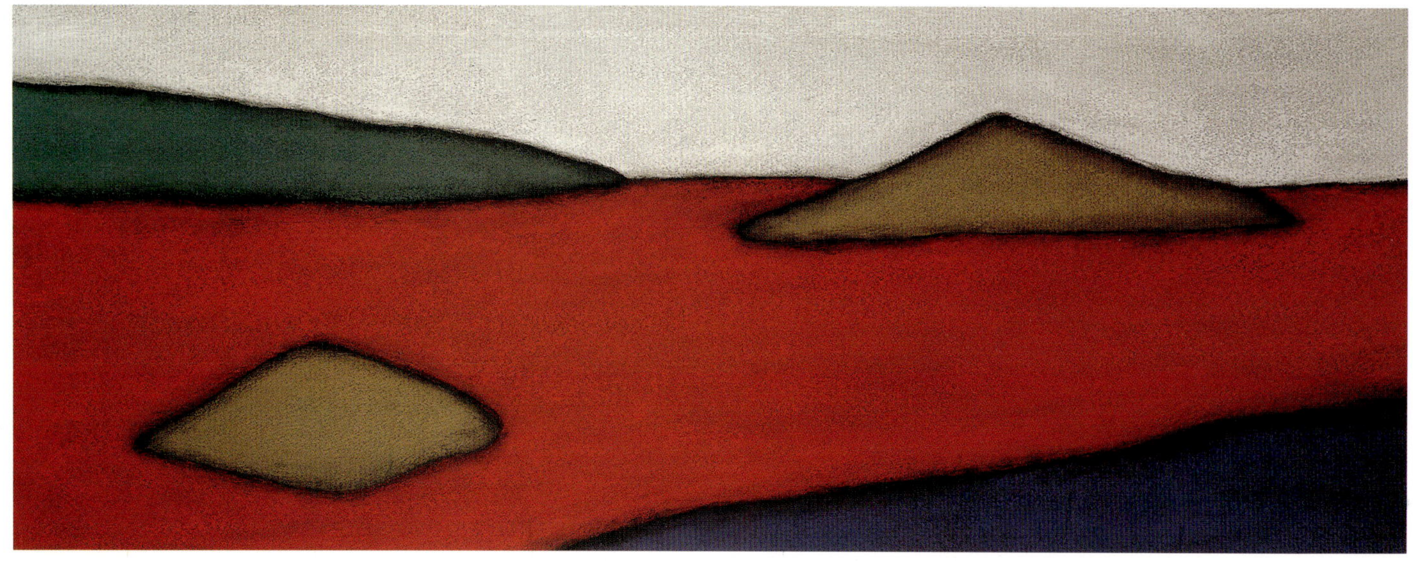

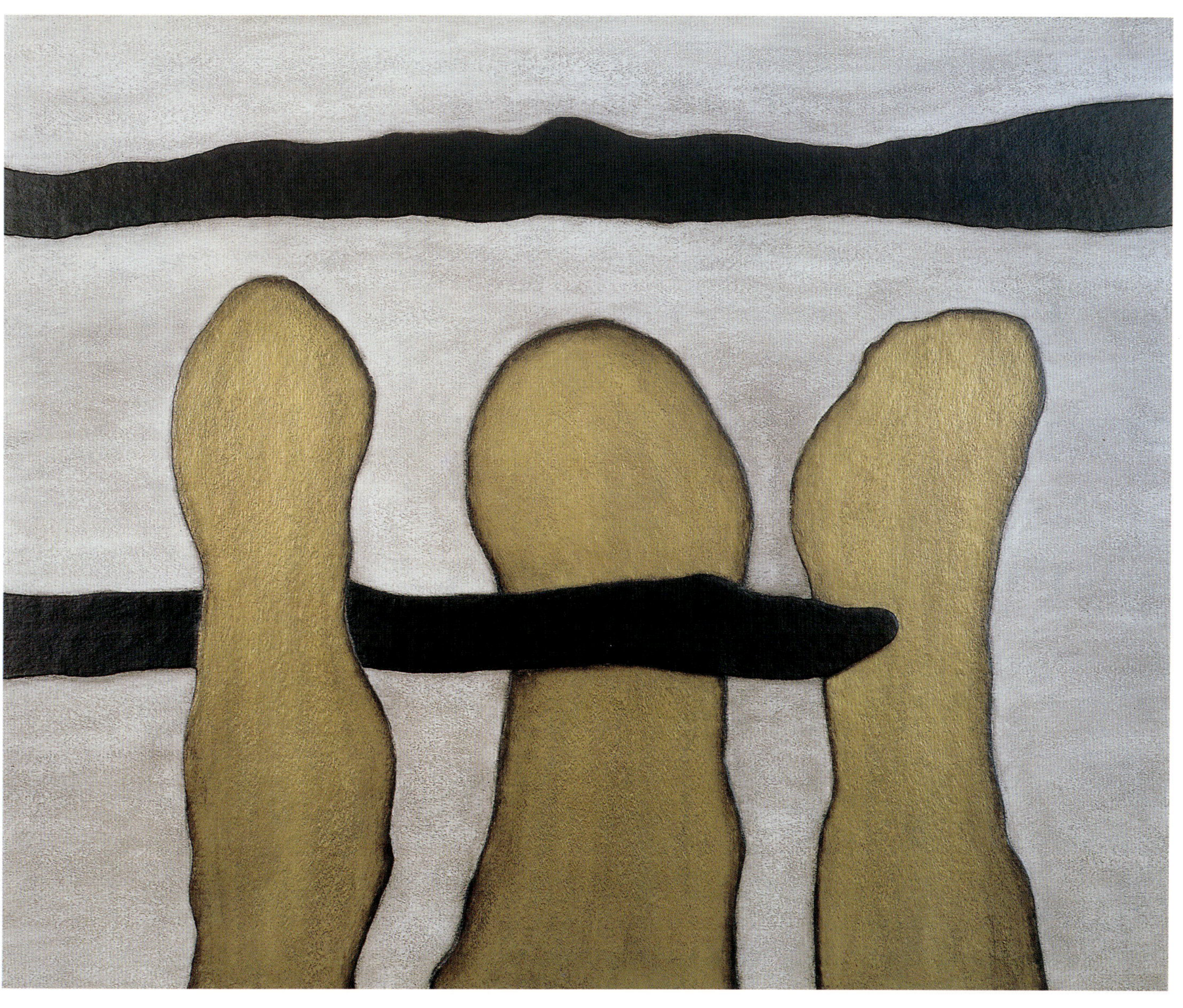

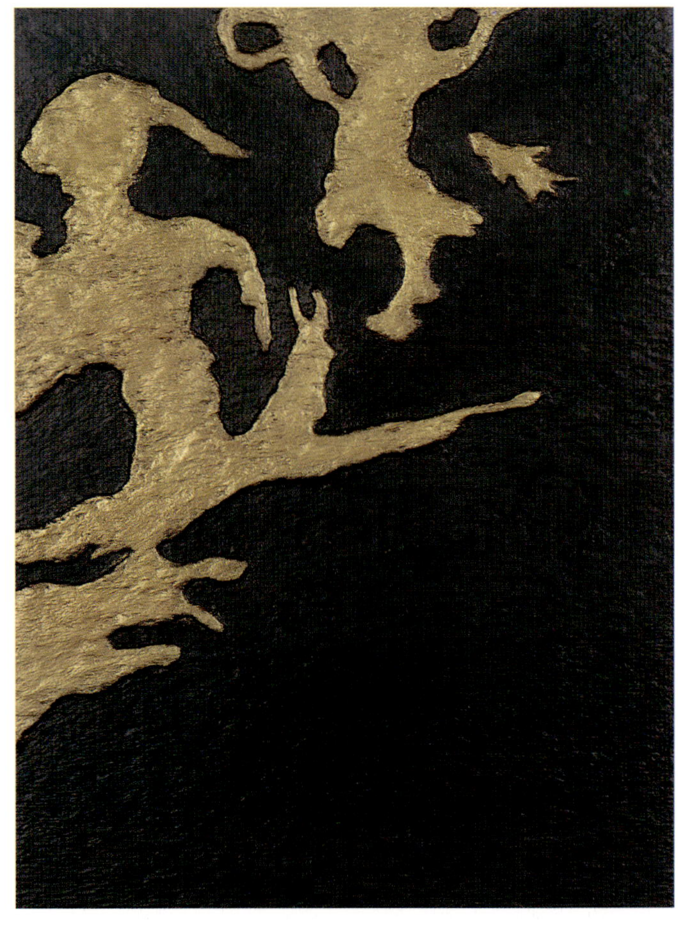

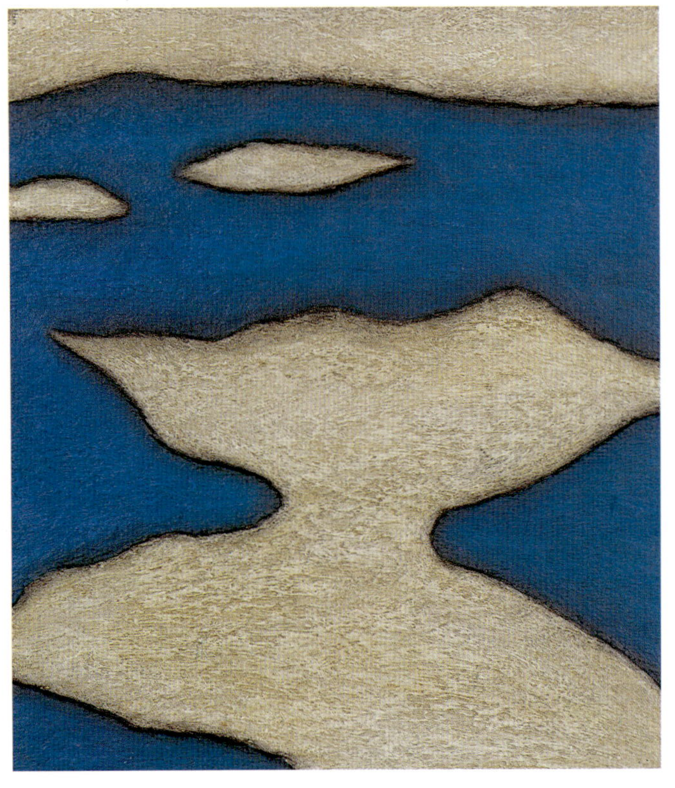

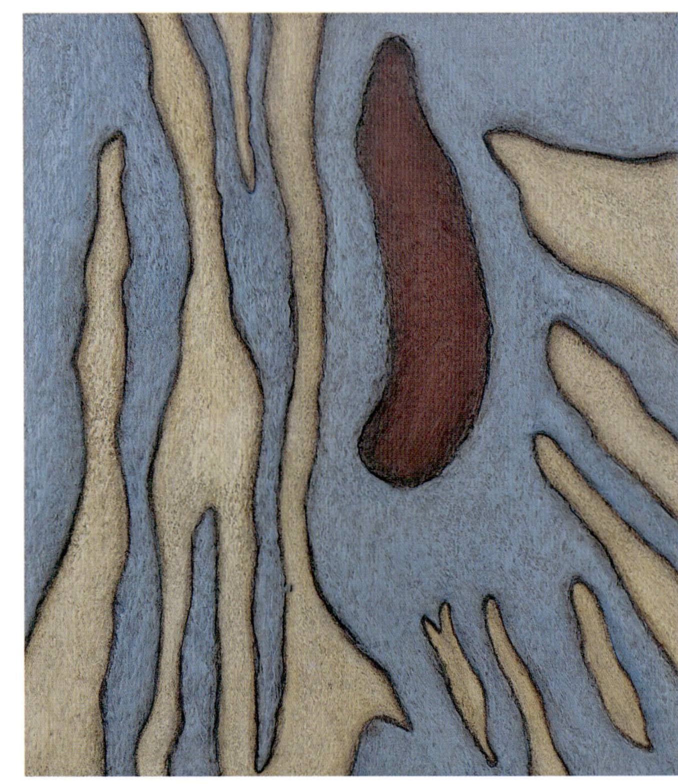

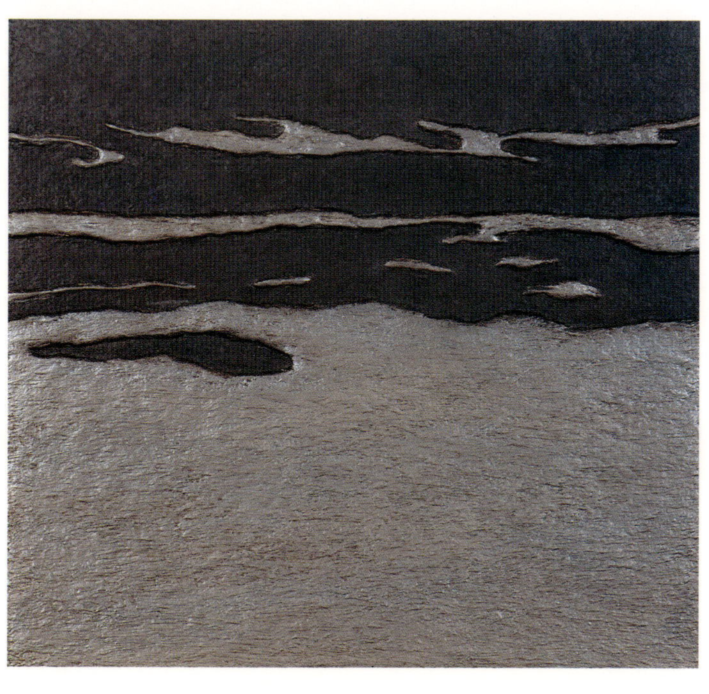

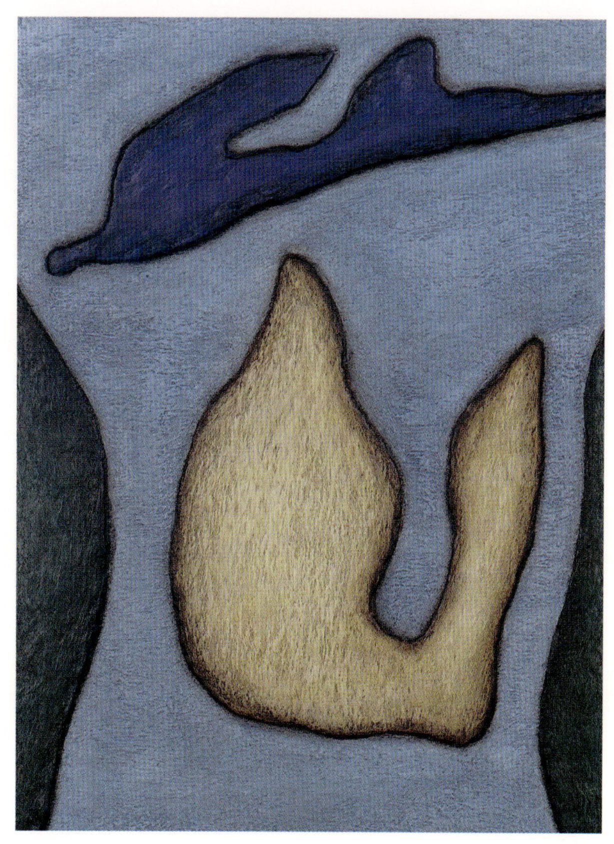

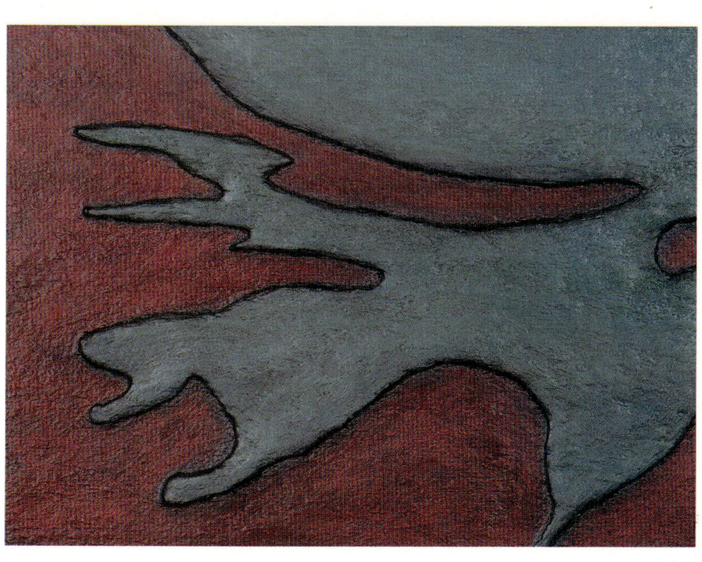

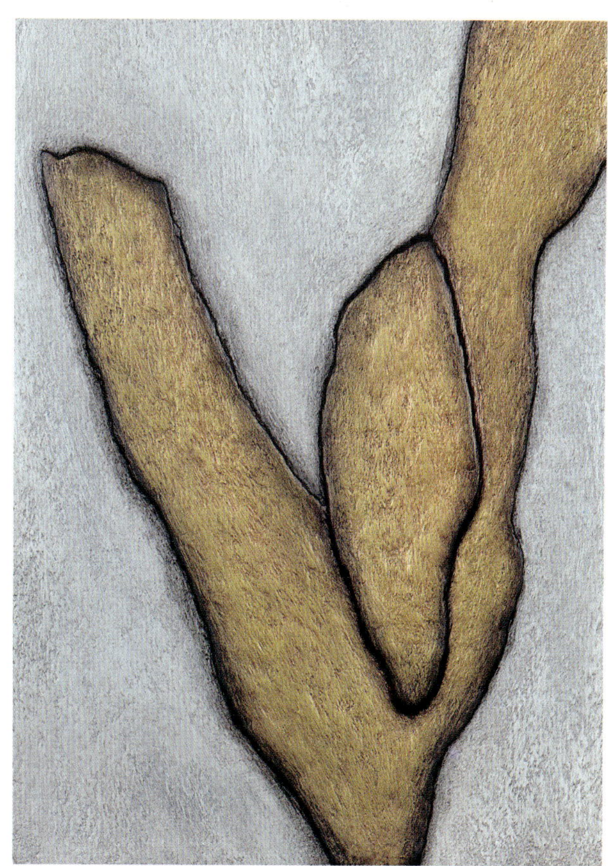

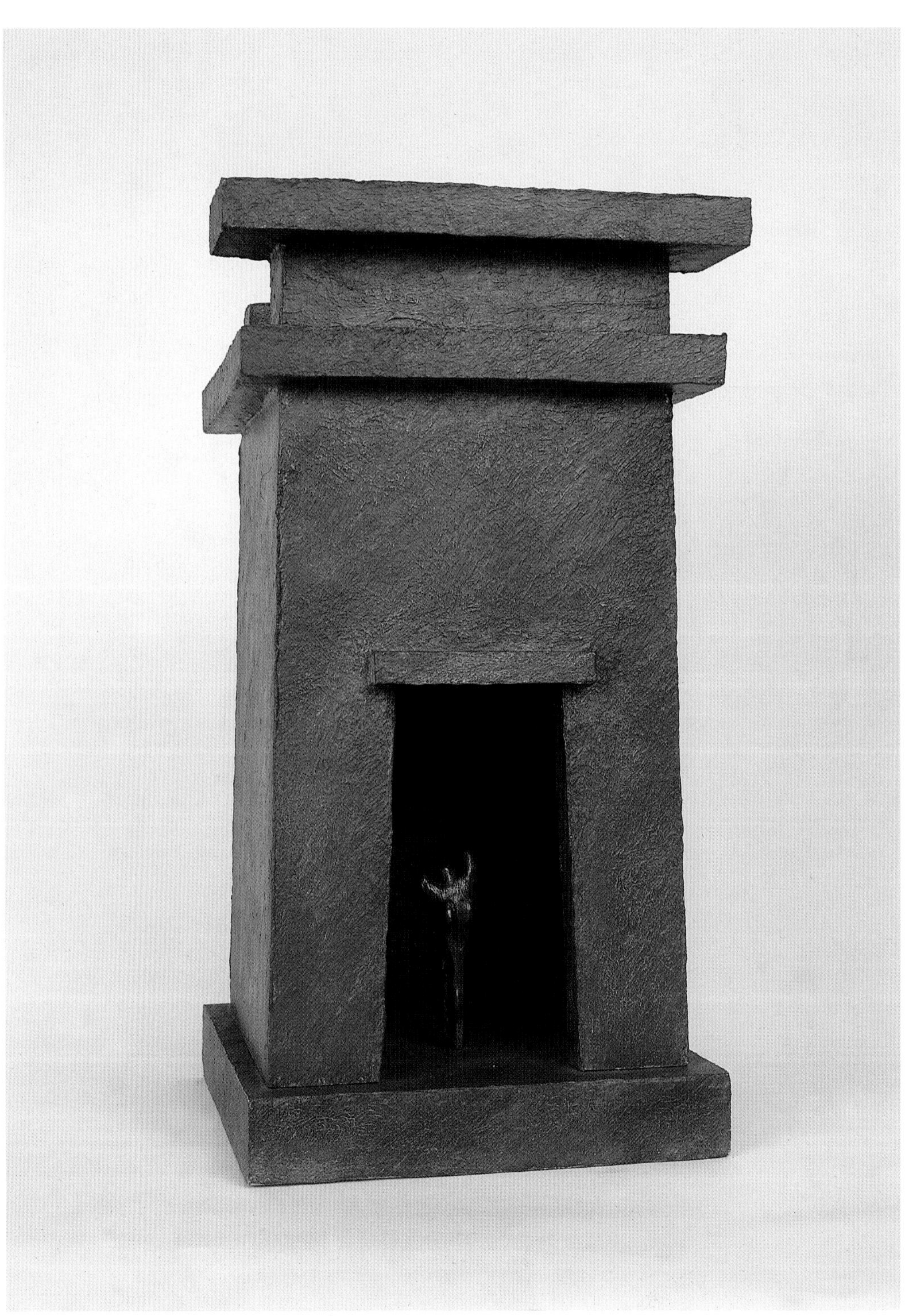

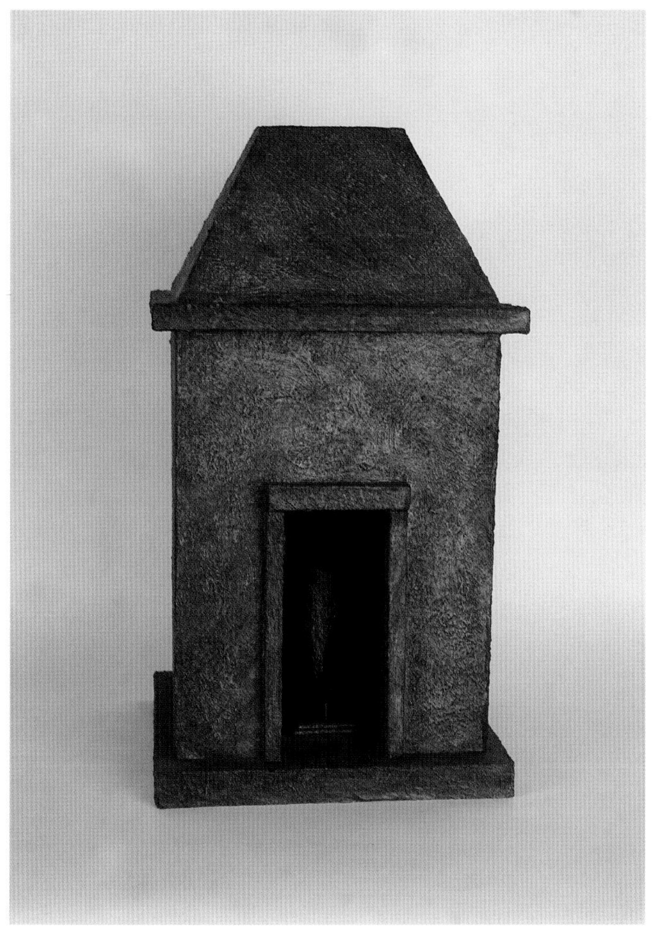

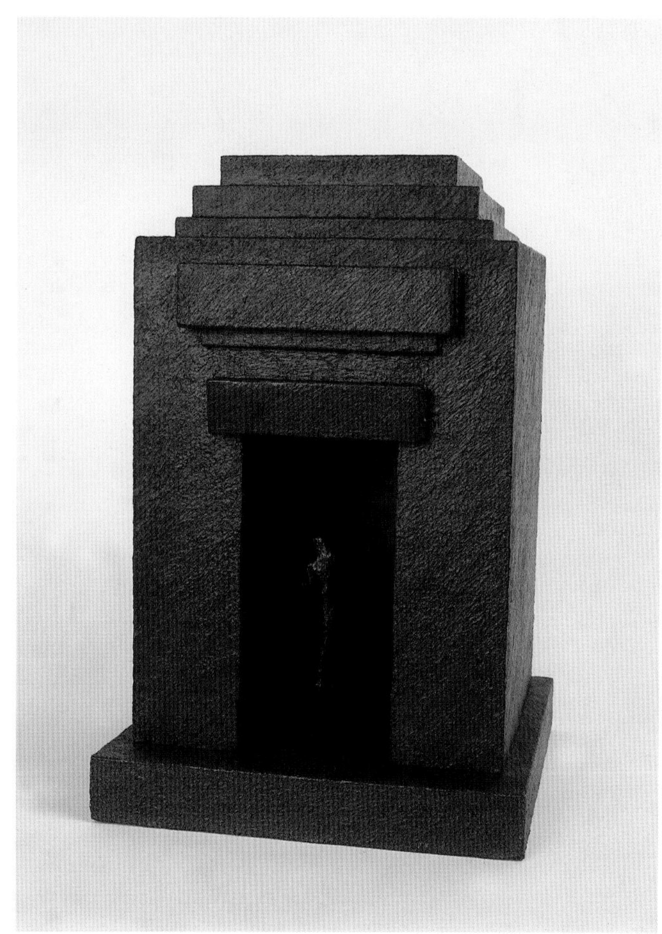

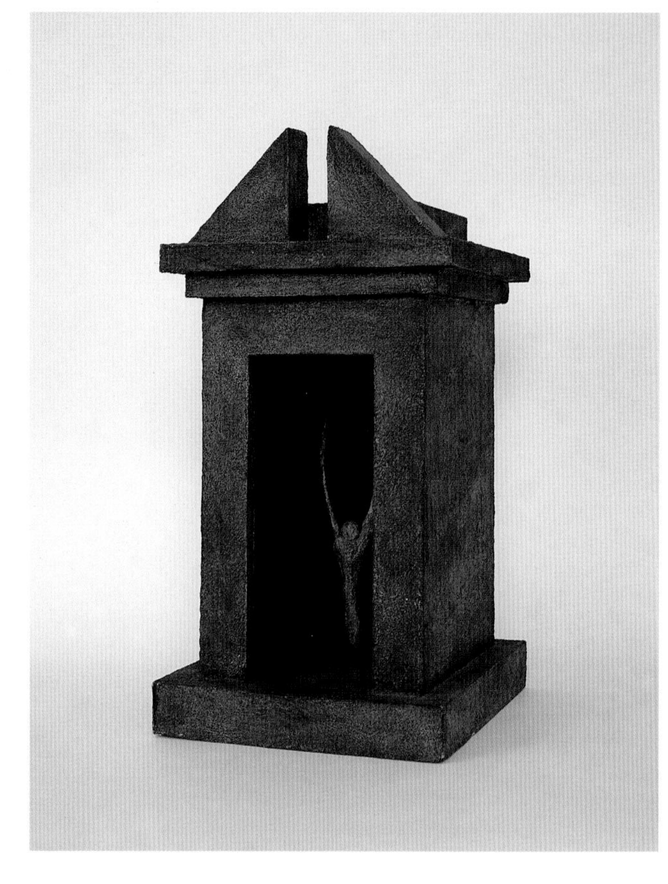

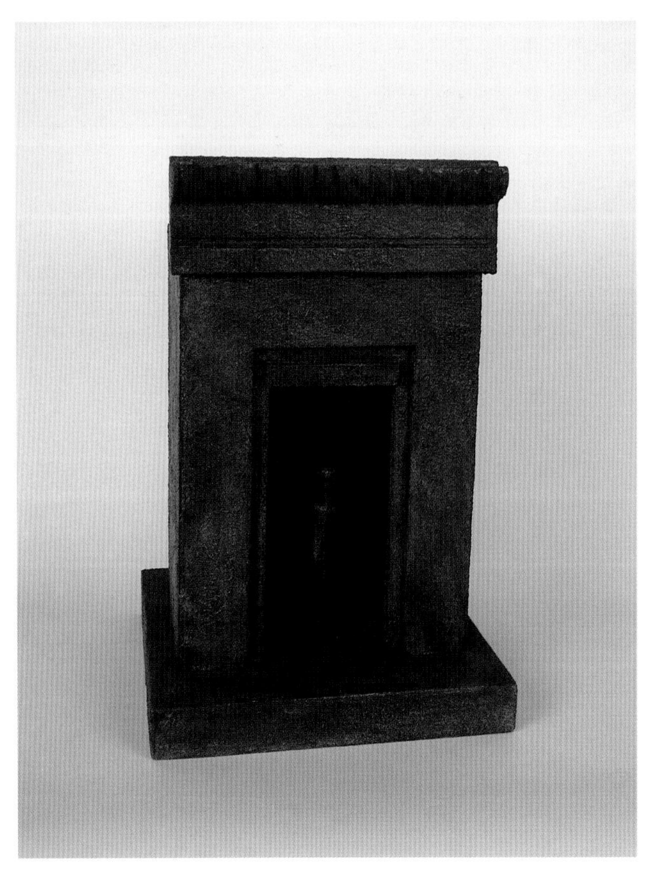

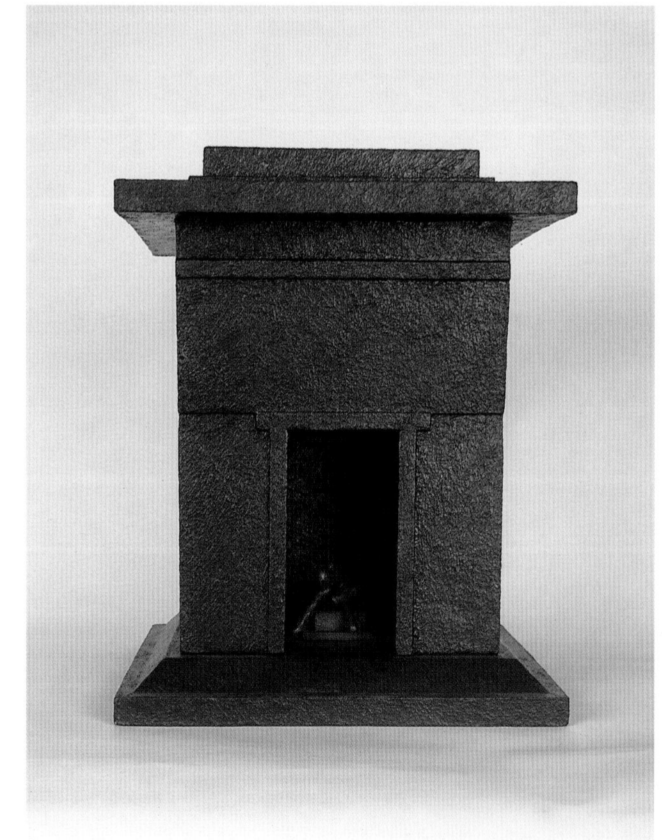

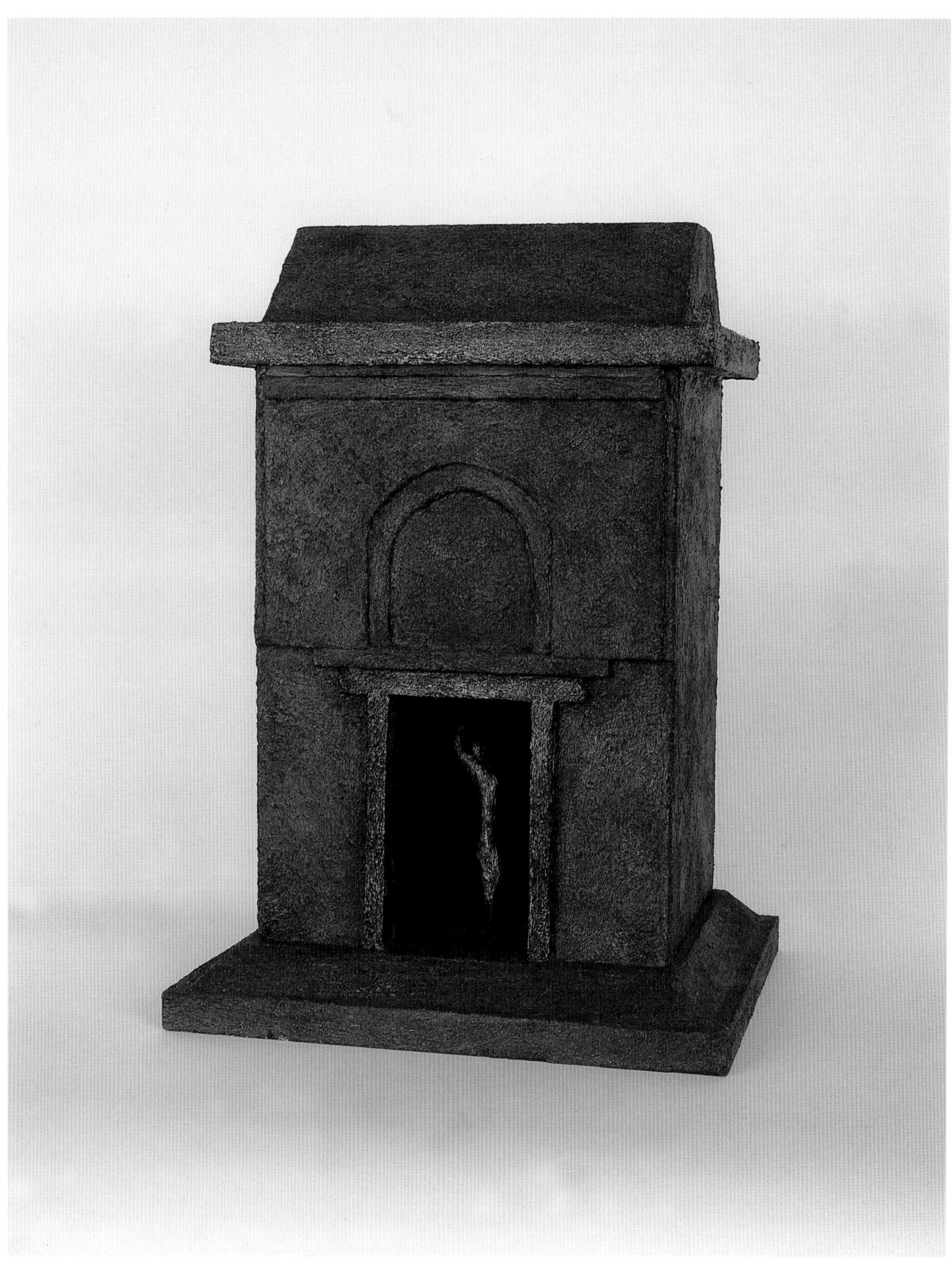

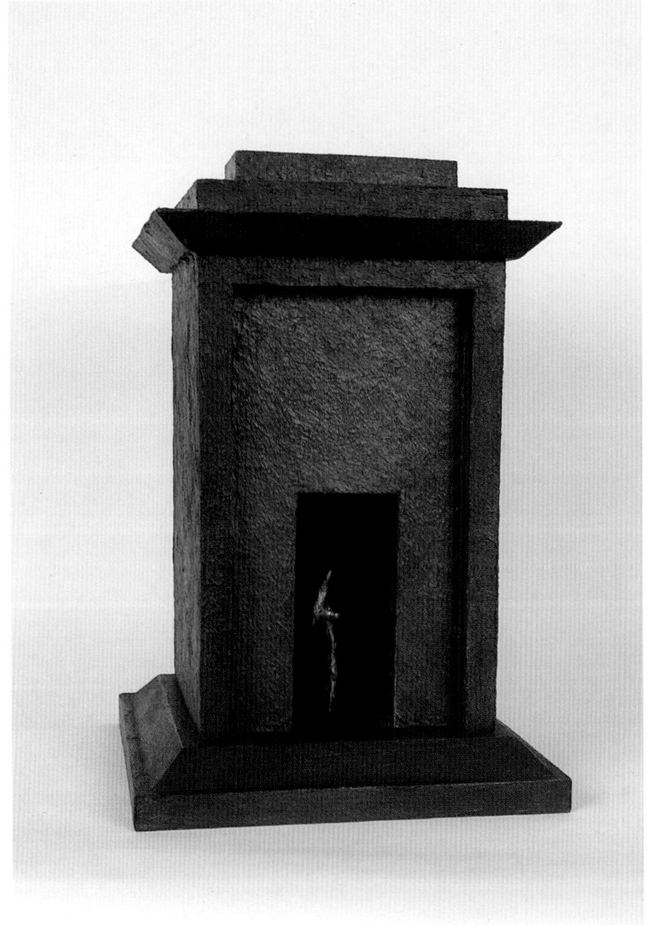

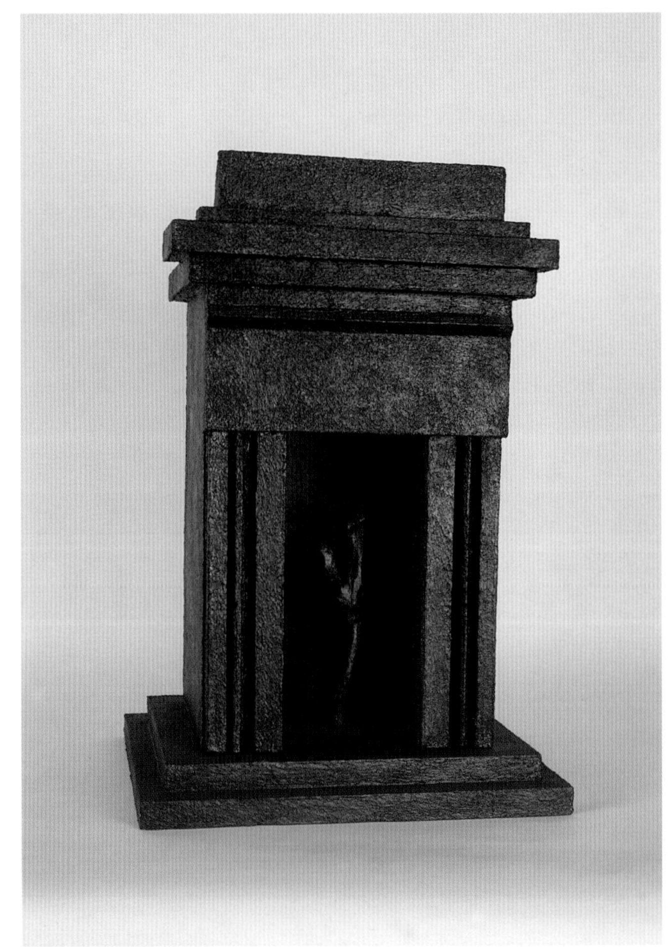

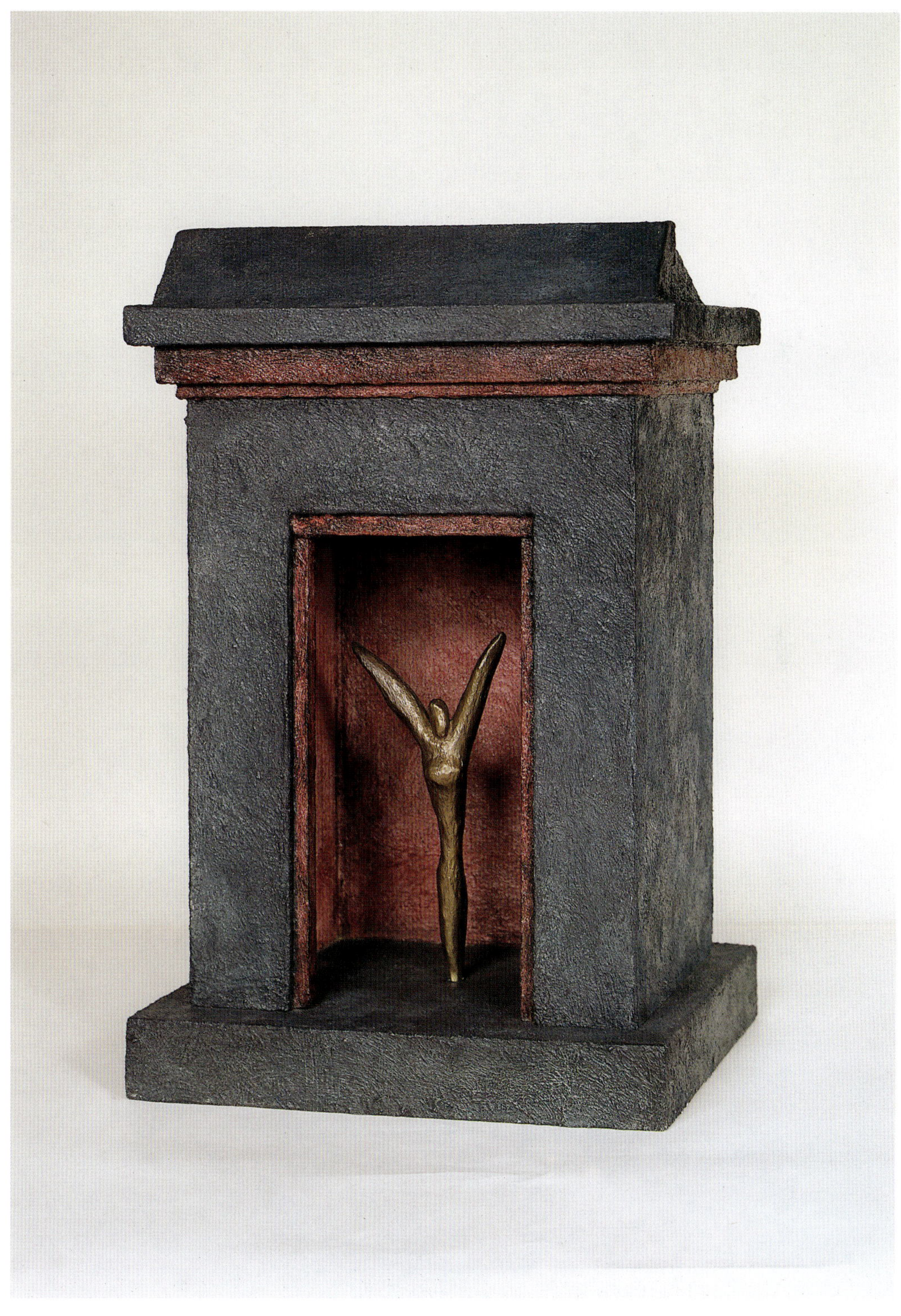

Catalogue of the Exhibition

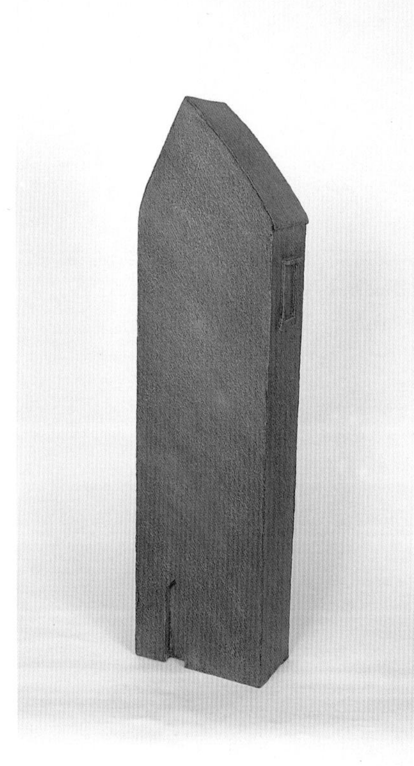

Ryel, 1981
cat. 38

PAINTINGS

1

Azba II, 1984
Acrylic on canvas over wood
64 x 48
74$^{3}/_{4}$ x 59 (framed)
Private collection
Illustrated p. 39

2

Iza II, 1984
Acrylic on canvas over wood
48 x 73$^{3}/_{4}$
59 x 84 (framed)
The Solomon R. Guggenheim Museum,
New York
Illustrated p. 19

3

Giro III, 1985
Acrylic on canvas over wood
48 x 84
59$^{1}/_{2}$ x 95$^{1}/_{2}$ (framed)
The Jewish Museum, New York
Illustrated p. 38

4

Isa, 1985
Acrylic on panel
13 x 9$^{1}/_{4}$
18$^{3}/_{4}$ x 15 (framed)
Collection of the artist
Illustrated p. 40

5

Avat II, 1985
Acrylic on canvas over wood
33$^{1}/_{2}$ x 47$^{3}/_{4}$
43 x 57$^{1}/_{4}$ (framed)
Private collection
Illustrated p. 41

6

Mazi, 1986
Acrylic on canvas over wood
48 x 72
59 x 83 (framed)
Swiss Bank Corporation
Illustrated p. 42

7

Natah, 1987
Acrylic on canvas over three panels
48 x 70
50$^{7}/_{8}$ x 72$^{7}/_{8}$ (framed)
Private collection, Palm Beach, Florida
Illustrated p. 28

8

Ara-Ilam, 1987
Acrylic on canvas over wood
33 x 48
36$^{1}/_{2}$ x 51$^{1}/_{2}$ (framed)
Private collection, New York
Illustrated p. 43

9

Dakayah, 1987
Acrylic on panel
23 $^1/_4$ x 30 $^3/_4$
28 x 35 $^1/_2$ (framed)
Private collection
Illustrated p. 44

10

Orev, 1987
Acrylic on board
18 $^1/_2$ x 13
24 $^3/_4$ x 19 $^1/_4$ (framed)
Collection of Nessa Rapoport
Illustrated p. 47

11

Otza II, 1987
Acrylic on canvas over wood
60 x 48
71 x 59 x 4 (framed)
Collection of
Drs. Bonnie Maslin and Yehuda Nir
Illustrated p. 46

12

Keba, 1988
Acrylic on board
30 x 22 $^1/_2$
Collection of the artist on loan to
Museum of Contemporary Religious Art,
Saint Louis University, Missouri
Illustrated p. 45

13

Ajyla, 1988
Acrylic on board
30 x 22 $^1/_2$
Collection of Idee German Schoenheimer
Illustrated p. 48

14

Yuna, 1988
Acrylic on canvas over wood
48 x 60
60 x 72 (framed)
Collection of Clyde Hershan
Illustrated p. 20

15

Tzyla, 1988
Acrylic on board
36 x 11
Collection of
Arlene and Howard Eisenberg
Illustrated p. 49

16

Ehlak II, 1988
Acrylic on canvas over wood
60 x 48
71 $^1/_2$ x 59 $^1/_2$ x 4 (framed)
Private collection, Palm Beach, Florida
Illustrated p. 50

17

Ozsef, 1989
Acrylic on canvas over board
60 x 48
69 $^1/_4$ x 57 $^1/_4$ x 4 (framed)
Collection of the artist
Illustrated p. 8

18

Rigua, 1989
Acrylic on board
22 x 26 $^1/_4$
Collection of
Rose and Morton Landowne, New York
Illustrated p. 52

19

Sido, 1989
Acrylic on board
22 x 15
Collection of Elysa Lazar
Illustrated p. 51

20

El-Kudeh, 1989
Acrylic on canvas over wood
48 x 60
57 $^1/_4$ x 69 $^1/_4$ x 4 (framed)
Private collection
Illustrated p. 31

21

Lyje, 1991
Acrylic on board
32 x 12 x 1 $^3/_4$
Collection of Hilde and Sidney Schonfeld
Illustrated p. 27

22

Yganh, 1991
Acrylic on canvas over wood
70 x 24 x 2
Collection of the artist
Illustrated p. 53

23

Tyhnu, 1991
Acrylic on board
12 x 32 x 1 $^3/_4$
Private collection
Illustrated p. 54

24

Ixqua, 1992
Acrylic on board
18 x 48 x 2
Collection of Andrea and Robert Hershan
Illustrated p. 54

25

Ilica, 1993
Acrylic on canvas over wood
24 x 70 x 2
Colby College Museum of Art,
Waterville, Maine
Museum purchase from the
Jetté Art Acquisition Fund
Illustrated p. 56

26

Rigu-Saar, 1993
Acrylic on canvas over wood
50 x 40 x 2
Collection of Leonard A. Kestenbaum,
Lawrence, New York
Illustrated as frontispiece

27

Orrah, 1993
Acrylic on wood
18 x 48 x 2
Courtesy of New Amsterdam Brewing
Company and the artist
Illustrated p. 56

28

Almah II, 1993
Acrylic on canvas over wood
58 x 72 x 2 $^1/_2$
Collection of the artist
Illustrated p. 10

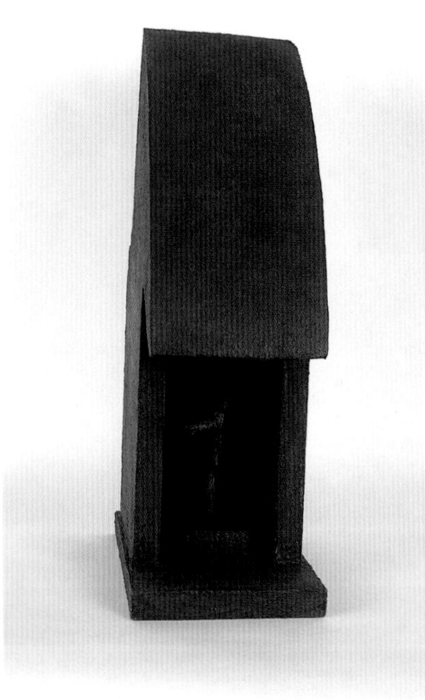

Ayin, 1983
cat. 42

29

Luzzan, 1993
Acrylic on canvas over wood
50 x 40 x 2
Private collection
Illustrated p. 22

30

Yshaar, 1994
Acrylic on canvas over wood
48 x 60 x 2$^{1}/_{2}$
Private collection
Illustrated p. 26

31

Naahm-Hwa, 1994
Acrylic on canvas over wood
40 x 50 x 2$^{1}/_{2}$
Collection of the artist
Illustrated p. 55

32

Madai, 1995
Acrylic on canvas over wood
72 x 48 x 2$^{1}/_{2}$
Private collection
Illustrated p. 23

33

Ohalim, 1995
Acrylic on canvas over wood
50 x 40 x 2$^{1}/_{2}$
Collection of the artist
Illustrated p. 32

34

Ornat, 1995
Acrylic on canvas over wood
40 x 50 x 2$^{1}/_{4}$
Private collection
Illustrated p. 24

35

Terhia, 1995
Acrylic on canvas over wood
48 x 34 x 2$^{1}/_{4}$
Collection of the artist

36

Ylyr, 1995
Acrylic on canvas over wood
48 x 60 x 2$^{1}/_{2}$
Collection of Idee German Schoenheimer
Illustrated p. 57

37

Eyda, 1995
(An installation of 7 paintings)
Acrylic on canvas over wood
Varying in size from
8 x 10 x 3 to 12 x 9 x 3
Mitchell Investment Management
Company, Inc.
Illustrated pp. 58–59

SCULPTURE

38

Ryel, 1981
Acrylic on wood and masonite
37 x 9$^{1}/_{2}$ x 5$^{3}/_{4}$
Collection of the artist
Illustrated p. 66

39

Moad, 1982
Acrylic on wood and masonite
46$^{3}/_{4}$ x 9$^{3}/_{4}$ x 8$^{1}/_{4}$
Collection of the artist
Illustrated p. 36

40

Layra, 1982
Acrylic on wood, bronze with patina
15 x 6 x 7
Private collection

41

Leba, 1983
Acrylic on wood
11 x 5$^{1}/_{2}$ x 6$^{7}/_{8}$
Private collection
Illustrated p. 6

42

Ayin, 1983
Acrylic on wood, bronze with patina
17 x 6 x 7
Private collection

43

Subah, 1984
Acrylic on wood, bronze with patina
9$^{1}/_{2}$ x 7 x 6
Collection of the artist
Illustrated p. 69

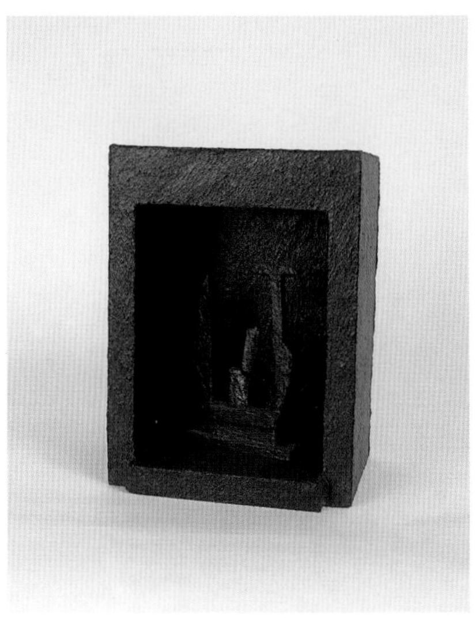

Subah, 1984
cat. 43

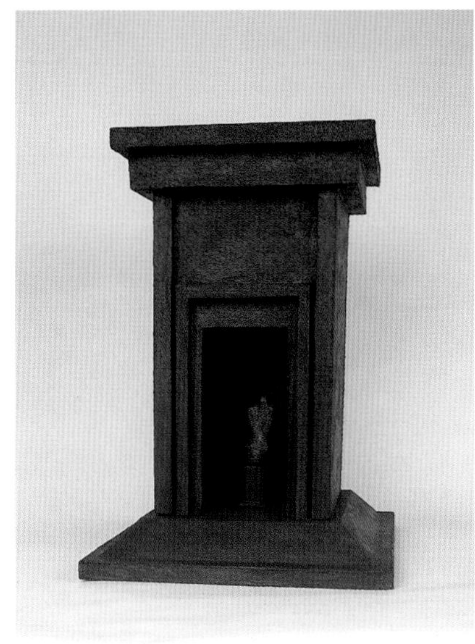

Itah, 1986
cat. 50

44

Alish, 1984
Acrylic on wood, bronze with patina
$14^{1}/_{2}$ x $8^{1}/_{8}$ x $8^{1}/_{8}$
Collection of Ellen and Herbert Kahn
Illustrated p. 61

45

Sorahi, 1984
Acrylic on wood, bronze with patina
$15^{3}/_{4}$ x $11^{1}/_{4}$ x $9^{3}/_{4}$
Collection of
Georgene S. and Irving H. Dreishpoon
Illustrated p. 63

46

Shani, 1984
Acrylic on wood, bronze with patina
$14^{3}/_{4}$ x 11 x $10^{1}/_{4}$
Private collection
Illustrated p. 64

47

Kanaf, 1985
Acrylic on wood, bronze with patina
$18^{1}/_{4}$ x $9^{1}/_{4}$ x $10^{1}/_{8}$
Private collection
Illustrated p. 62

48

Brun, 1985
Acrylic on wood, bronze with patina
21 x 12 x $9^{1}/_{4}$
Collection of the artist
Illustrated p. 13

49

Ashta, 1985
Acrylic on wood, bronze with patina
$18^{1}/_{4}$ x $12^{1}/_{2}$ x 11
Private collection
Illustrated p. 64

50

Itah, 1986
Acrylic on wood, bronze with patina
19 x 14 x 15
Private collection

51

Lifanah, 1985
Acrylic on wood, bronze with patina
$16^{5}/_{8}$ x $10^{3}/_{4}$ x $10^{1}/_{2}$
Collection of the artist on loan to
Museum of Contemporary Religious Art,
Saint Louis University, Missouri
Illustrated p. 65

52

Rydda, 1985
Acrylic on wood, bronze with patina
$16^{1}/_{8}$ x $8^{1}/_{2}$ x $9^{1}/_{8}$
Private collection
Illustrated p. 60

53

Imti, 1985
Acrylic on wood, bronze with patina
$16^{7}/_{8}$ x 11 x $12^{1}/_{2}$
Collection of Douglas F. Maxwell
Illustrated p. 62

54

Eykhal, 1985
Acrylic on wood, bronze with patina
15 x 12 x $10^{1}/_{2}$
Collection of Josh Rapoport Kahn and
Mattie Rapoport Kahn
Illustrated p. 62

55

Ollu, 1985
Acrylic on wood, bronze with patina
$15^{1}/_{2}$ x $10^{1}/_{2}$ x $10^{1}/_{2}$
Collection of Karen Lehmann Eisner and
David F. Eisner
Illustrated p. 61

56

Ziba II, 1987
Acrylic on wood
86 x $19^{1}/_{2}$ x $13^{7}/_{8}$
Private collection
Illustrated p. 15

57

Shalev, 1994
Bronze with patina
No. 6 of an edition of 7
$8^{1}/_{8}$ x 6 x $3^{1}/_{4}$
Private collection

Chronology

<table>
<tr><td>1952</td><td>Born May 8th, New York. Son of Ellen (neé Schapiro) and Herbert Kahn, and the younger brother of Felice Kahn (now Felice Kahn Zisken).</td></tr>
<tr><td>1958–1966</td><td>Attends Samson Raphael Hirsh Elementary School, New York.</td></tr>
<tr><td>1966–1970</td><td>Attends Manhattan Talmudic Academy High School, New York.</td></tr>
<tr><td>1970–1971</td><td>Attends Tel Aviv University, Israel.</td></tr>
<tr><td>1971–1974</td><td>Travels extensively through the Middle East, Europe, Australia and Africa. Studies at Har Etzion Seminary in Israel.</td></tr>
<tr><td>1974–1976</td><td>Graduates from Hunter College with B.A., summa cum laude and kappa pi. Receives the Estelle Levy Award for Outstanding Merit in Art, as well as the Herman Muehlstein Foundation Graduate School Award.</td></tr>
<tr><td>1976–1978</td><td>Enters Pratt Institute, Masters Degree Program, Brooklyn, New York. Receives internship, Art Program, Pratt Institute (1977). Receives Pratt Institute Fellowship Award in Painting (1978). Graduates from Pratt Institute with M.F.A. in 1978.

Adjunct Lecturer, New York Technical College, City University of New York, Brooklyn (through 1985).

Leases studio in Long Island City with four other artists, including painter Sharon Florin, with whom he continues to share a studio.</td></tr>
<tr><td>1979</td><td>First solo exhibition at Fordham University.

Artist-in-residence, Kaufman Cultural Center, New York (through 1985).</td></tr>
<tr><td>1981</td><td>First museum group show at The Queens Museum, Flushing, New York.</td></tr>
<tr><td>1983</td><td>Solo exhibition, Althea Viafora Gallery, New York (1984, 1986, 1987, 1989).

Starts gallery and art museum lecture series for a group of collectors through the Jewish Community Center on the Palisades (until the present).</td></tr>
<tr><td>1984</td><td>The Solomon R. Guggenheim Museum is gifted Iza II for its permanent collection.</td></tr>
</table>

| 1985 | Seventeen paintings and two sculptures included in *New Horizons in American Art: 1985 Exxon National Exhibition*, Solomon R. Guggenheim Museum, New York.

Visiting artist, Mishkenot Sha'Ananim, Jerusalem, Israel. |

| 1986 | Marries writer Nessa Rapoport, April 10.

Begins to teach painting at the School of Visual Arts, New York (until the present).

"*Hoya*," an edition of thirty-six etchings, is commissioned and published by the Jewish Theological Seminary of America. *Isa* appears on the cover of *Tikkun* magazine. |

| 1988 | Solo exhibition at Mary Ryan Gallery, New York (1991, 1993, 1995, 1997); and Gloria Luria Gallery, Bay Harbor Islands, Florida (1990, 1992).

Creates set for Solomons Dance Company, *Aspen Grove* and *Bone Yard*, premiered at the Joyce Theater and St. Mark's Church, New York.

Son Joshua is born, May 10. |

| 1989–1990 | Creates set for Elizabeth Swados, *Song of Songs*, premiered at Central Synagogue; and for Muna Tseng, *Aluat-El*, premiered at Riverside Park, New York.

Creates set for Elizabeth Swados, *Jonah*, premiered at the Public Theater; and for Muna Tseng, *Ways, Shrines, Mysteries*, premiered at Florence Gould Hall, both New York. |

| 1991–1993 | Daughter Mattie is born, March 17, 1992.

Creates first monumental outdoor sculpture, *Shalev*, bronze and stone, commissioned by Jane Owen and the Robert Lee Blaffer Trust for New Harmony, Indiana. Designs the label for New Amsterdam Brewing Company's Winter Anniversary Limited Edition. |

| 1994–1996 | Commissioned by the Nathan Cummings Foundation to execute *The Twelve Tribes* and *Creation of the World*, a series of twelve works on paper and one painting for the Jewish Family Congregation, South Salem, New York. Creates installation of seven paintings, titled *Eyda*, commissioned by Mitchell Investment Management Company, Inc., Boston, Massachussets. *Rigu-Saar* appears on the cover of *Collected Writings of Adrienne Rich* (New York: Quality Paperback Book Club, 1994).

Study for Doekh appears on the cover of *The American Journal of Pathology* (January 1996). Originally commissioned by Dr. Mark Tykocinski for his article, "Antigen-Presenting Cell Engineering." |

| 1997 | Creates *Gan Hazikaron: Garden of Remembrance*, an outdoor installation of five bronzes as Holocaust memorial for the Jewish Community Center on the Palisades. Commissioned by Holocaust survivors and their children. |

Selected Exhibitions

Solo Exhibitions

1979	Fordham University, New York.
1980	Robert Brown, New York.
1981	Blumberg Harris, New York.
1983	Althea Viafora Gallery, New York (1984, 1986, 1987, 1989).
1985	Bernard Jacobson, Ltd., Los Angeles, California.
	J. Robert Fisher Hall at Mishkenot Sha'Ananim, Jerusalem, Israel.
1987	Krygier/Landau Contemporary Art, Los Angeles, California.
	John Berggruen Gallery, San Francisco, California.
	Philadelphia Museum of Judaica, Philadelphia, Pennsylvania.
1988	Harcus Gallery, Boston, Massachusetts.
	Cleveland Center for Contemporary Art, Cleveland, Ohio (1993).
	Mary Ryan Gallery, New York (1991, 1993, 1995, 1997).
	Gloria Luria Gallery, Bay Harbor Islands, Florida (1990, 1992).
1990	Marilyn Butler Fine Art, Scottsdale, Arizona.
1993	Thomson Gallery, Minneapolis, Minnesota.
	Litwin Gallery, Wichita, Kansas.
1994	Allene Lapides Gallery, Santa Fe, New Mexico.
1995	Andrea Marquit Fine Arts, Boston, Massachusetts.
1996	The Warehouse Gallery, Lee, Massachusetts.
	Harmon-Meek Gallery, Naples, Florida.
1997	The Hyde Collection, Glens Falls, New York.

1980   Zolla/Lieberman, Chicago, Illinois.

1981   *Annual Juried Exhibition*, Queens Museum, Queens, New York. Curated by John Perreault (catalogue).

1983   *Saints*, Harm Boukaert Gallery, New York.

1984   *From the Abstract to the Image*, Oscarsson Hood Gallery, New York.

2500 Sculptors Across America, Civilian Warfare, New York.

1985   *Contemporary Sculpture on a Pedestal*. Originated at the Moody Gallery, University of Alabama. Traveled to University Galleries, University of South Florida; and Huntsville Museum of Art, Huntsville, Alabama. Curated by Susan L. Halper (catalogue).

New Horizons in American Art: 1985 Exxon National Exhibition, Solomon R. Guggenheim Museum, New York. Curated by Lisa Dennison (catalogue).

The Doll and Figurine Show, The Hillwood Art Gallery, Long Island University, New York. Curated by Judy Collischan Van Wagner and Carol Becker Davis (catalogue).

Between Drawing and Sculpture, Sculpture Center, New York. Curated by Douglas Dreishpoon (catalogue).

Drawings, Cleveland Center for Contemporary Art, Cleveland, Ohio.

1986   *Anchorage/New York: Small Sculpture*, Visual Arts Center of Anchorage, Anchorage, Alaska. Curated by David Donihue (catalogue).

Jewish Themes: Contemporary American Artists Part II, The Jewish Museum, New York. Curated by Susan T. Goodman (catalogue).

Landscape in the Age of Anxiety, Lehman Art College, Bronx, New York. Curated by Nina Castelli Sundell. Traveled to The Cleveland Center for Contemporary Art, Cleveland, Ohio (catalogue).

A View of Nature, The Aldrich Museum, Ridgefield, Connecticut. Curated by Ellen O'Donnell (catalogue).

1987   *Emerging Artists 1978–1986: Selections from the Exxon Series*, Solomon R. Guggenheim Museum, New York. Curated by Diane Waldman (catalogue).

The New Romantic Landscape, Whitney Museum of American Art, Fairfield County Branch, Stamford, Connecticut.

Sacred Spaces, Everson Museum of Art, Syracuse, New York. Curated by Dominique Nahas (catalogue).

Contemporary American Landscape: Reflections of Social Change, Summit Art Center, Summit, New Jersey. Curated by Nancy Cohen, Kiku Fukui and Liz Kelsey.

1988   *Art on Paper*, Weatherspoon Art Gallery, The University of North Carolina at Greensboro (catalogue).

Dia de los Muertos, Alternative Museum, New York (catalogue).

Golem! Danger, Deliverance and Art, The Jewish Museum, New York. Curated by Emily Bilski (catalogue).

Annual Juried Show, Queens Museum, New York. Curated by Irving Sandler (catalogue).

1989   *Rugged Terrain: Landscape Painting*, Shea & Beker, New York.

Contemporary Landscape: Five Views, Waterworks Visual Arts Center, Salisbury, Virginia. Curated by J. Moore (catalogue).

Monotypes, The Cleveland Center for Contemporary Art, Cleveland, Ohio.

1990   *Southeast Bank Collects: A Florida Corporation Views Contemporary Art.* Organized by the Norton Gallery of Art, West Palm Beach, Florida. Traveled to the Bass Museum of Art, Miami Beach, Florida; Museum of Fine Arts, St. Petersburg, Florida; Polk Museum of Art, Lakeland, Florida; and Samuel P. Harn Museum of Art, Gainesville, Florida (catalogue).

Horizons, Pfizer, Inc., through The Art Advisors, The Museum of Modern Art, New York.

Insistent Landscapes, Security Pacific Gallery, Los Angeles, California. Curated by Mark Johnstone (catalogue).

1991   *Retrieving the Elemental Form*, Schmidt-Bingham Gallery, New York. Traveled to Lakeview Museum of Arts and Science, Peoria, Illinois; and Fresno Art Museum, Fresno, California (catalogue).

Playing Around: Toys by Artists, DeCordova Museum and Sculpture Park, Lincoln, Massachusetts.

1992   *Off the Wall*, Cleveland Center for Contemporary Art, Cleveland, Ohio.

ECO-92, Museum of Modern Art, Rio de Janeiro, Brazil (catalogue).

Contemporary American Painting and Sculpture, Art in Embassies, U.S. Department of State, American Embassy, Tel Aviv, Israel. Curated by Louise Eliasof and Renne Du Pont Harrison.

1993   *Timely Timeless*, Aldrich Museum, Ridgefield, Connecticut. Curated by Douglas F. Maxwell (catalogue).

25 Years, Cleveland Center for Contemporary Art, Cleveland, Ohio. Curated by Majorie Talalay.

Aspects of Sculpture, The Ulrich Museum of Art, Wichita, Kansas. Curated by Donald Knaub.

Sanctuaries: Recovering the Holy in Art, Museum of Contemporary Religious Art, Saint Louis University, St. Louis, Missouri. Curated by Terrence Dempsey.

1994   *A Bouquet for Juan*, Nancy Hoffman Gallery, New York.

Landscape Not Landscape, Gallery Camino Real, Boca Raton, Florida. Curated by Douglas F. Maxwell (catalogue).

1995   *Art on Paper*, The Weatherspoon Art Gallery, The University of North Carolina at Greensboro (catalogue).

Never Again, The Cathedral of St. John the Divine, New York. Curated by Noga Garrison.

Painting North, Art in Embassies, U.S. Department of State, American Embassy, Santiago, Chile (catalogue).

1996   *By the Sea*, Fotouhi Cramer Gallery, New York. Curated by Robert G. Edelman and Renee Fotouhi.

Destiny Manifest: American Landscape Painting in the Nineties, The Samuel P. Harn Museum of Art, Gainesville, Florida. Curated by Dede Young (catalogue).

The Figure in 20th Century Sculpture, Edwin A. Ulrich Museum of Art, Wichita, Kansas. Traveled to eleven venues in the United States.

Public Collections

Baer, Marks, Upham, New York
Chemical Bank, New York
Colby College Museum of Art, Waterville, Maine
Dreyfus Corporation, New York
Edwin A. Ulrich Museum of Art, Wichita, Kansas
Exxon Corporation, Miami, Florida
Fidelity Investments Corporation, Boston, Massachusetts
Fort Wayne Museum, Fort Wayne, Indiana
I.N.A. Museum, Cigna Corporation, Philadelphia, Pennsylvania
The Jewish Museum, New York
McCarter English, Newark, New Jersey
Mitchell Investment Management Company, Inc., Boston, Massachusetts
Progressive Corporation, Cleveland, Ohio
Prudential Insurance, New York
Rose Art Museum, Brandeis University, Waltham, Massachusetts
Salomon Brothers, Inc., New York
Skadden, Arps, Slate, Neagher & Flom, New York
The Solomon R. Guggenheim Museum, New York
Swiss Bank Corporation, New York
Weatherspoon Art Gallery, The University of North Carolina at Greensboro

Selected Bibliography

1981   John Perreault, *Annual Juried Exhibition, 1981*, exh. cat., The Queens Museum, Flushing, New York.

1983   Michael Brenson, "Review," *The New York Times*, December 16, 1983, p. C30.

1984   Douglas Dreishpoon, "Review," *Arts Magazine*, January 1984, p. 7.

Grace Glueck, "Review," *The New York Times*, November 2, 1984, p. C25.

1985   Douglas Dreishpoon, "Essence of Vision: The Art of Tobi Kahn," *Arts Magazine*, January 1985, pp. 81–83.

Susan A. Harris, "Review," *Arts Magazine*, January 1985, p. 40.

Meg Perlman, "Review," *Art News*, April 1985, pp. 144–145.

Kristine McKenna, "Review," *Los Angeles Times*, May 3, 1985, section IV, p. 15.

Amei Wallach, "New Horizons in Guggenheim Exhibit," *New York Newsday*, September 15, 1985.

Michael Brenson, "Art: 'New Horizons' at the Guggenheim," *The New York Times*, September 20, 1985.

Theodore Wolff, "Promising Artists at Guggenheim," *Christian Science Monitor*, October 7, 1985.

Karin Lipson, "By Artists for Artists," *New York Newsday*, October 18, 1985.

Ellen Glassman, "Tobi Kahn is an Artist Who's Coming into His Own," *Pratt folio*, Fall 1985, pp. 6–7.

Jane Bell, "New Horizons in American Art," *Art News*, November 1985.

Judy Collischan Van Wagner, *The Doll Show*, exh. cat., Hillwood Art Gallery, C.W. Post, Long Island University, New York, 1985, p. 37.

Douglas Dreishpoon, *Between Drawing and Sculpture*, exh. cat., Sculpture Center, New York, 1985.

Judd Tully, "New Horizons in Art: Exxon's Best National," *Art World*, October 1985.

Michael Brenson, "Art: 8 Artists in 'Between Drawing and Sculpture,'" *The New York Times,* December 20, 1985, p. C29.

1986   Virginia Rembert, "Sculpture on a Pedestal," *Art Papers*, March/April 1986.

Amei Wallach, "Two Theme Shows: At the Guggenheim, At the Jewish," *New York Newsday*, July 25, 1986, p. 16.

Michael Brenson, "Bringing Fresh Approaches to Ages-Old Jewish Themes," *The New York Times*, August 3, 1986, p. 27.

Eleanor Heartney, "Review," *Art News*, October 1986, p. 148.

Robert G. Edelman, "Review," *Art in America*, October 1986, pp. 165–166.

1987   Douglas Dreishpoon, "Review," *Arts Magazine*, January 1987, p. 127.

Vivien Raynor, "Views of Nature on Exhibit at Ridgefield's Expanded Aldrich," *The New York Times* (Connecticut), January 11, 1987, p. 30.

Vivien Raynor, "Center for Visual Arts: Landscape as Reflections of Social Change," *The New York Times* (New Jersey), March 15, 1987, p. 30.

Eileen Watkins, "Inventive Landscapes Reflect Inner Visions in Jersey Center for Visual Arts Exhibit," *Newark Star Ledger*, March 1987, p. 24.

Kenneth Baker, "Review," *San Francisco Chronicle*, March 28, 1987, p. 37.

Colin Gardner, "Review," *Los Angeles Times*, May 22, 1987, part 6, p. 14.

David Bourdon, "For Spacious Skies," *House & Garden*, August, 1987, p. 44b.

Michael Brenson, "Review," *The New York Times*, November 6, 1987, p. C37.

1988   Susan Kandel, Elizabeth Hayt-Adkins, "Tobi Kahn," *Art News*, January 1988, p. 164.

Margaret Moorman, "The Multitude of Styles at the Queens Museum Show," *New York Newsday* (New York Weekend section), January 8, 1988, p. 21.

Leslie Judd Ahlander, "Miami Art Scene," *Miami News*, January 15, 1988, p. C3.

Helen Cullinan, "Our Collective Hang-Ups," *The Plain Dealer* (Cleveland, Ohio), February 22, 1988, p. 32.

Susan Mernit, "Artist Worth Watching: Tobi Kahn," *MD Magazine*, May 1988, pp. 35, 38, 43.

Vivian Raynor, "Tracking The Creative Process," *The New York Times* (Westchester), May 22, 1988, p. 26.

Alexandra Enders, "Openings," *Art and Antiques*, October, 1988, p. 52.

Michael Brenson, "Ambiguous Golem," *The New York Times,* section C, December 16, 1988.

1989   Paul Barringer, "Landscapes of Self vs. Picturesque Conventions," *The Arts Journal*, April 1989, p. 17.

Shaw Smith, "North Carolina, Contemporary Landscape: Five Views," *New Art Examiner*, May 1989, p. 52.

Michael Kimmelman, "Review," *The New York Times*, May 19, 1989, p. C33.

Suzanne Davis, "Contemporary Landscape, Five Views," *Atlanta Art Papers,* May / June 1989, pp. 57–58.

Ricardo Pau-Llosa, "A Convergence of Visual Cultures," *Art International,* Spring 1989, pp. 17–23.

Michael Brenson, "Rugged Terrain," *The New York Times*, June 23, 1989, p. C26.

1990   Susan Kleinman, "Making Mountains Skip," *Forward*, July 6, 1990, pp. 9–11.

James Magruder, "Call Me Leviathan," *The Village Voice*, April 3, 1990, p. 102.

Edith Newhall, "In The Belly of the Beast," *New York Magazine*, February 26, 1990, p. 36.

1991   Edith Newhall, "Review," *New York Magazine*, September 23, 1991, p. 61.

Deborah Solomon, "Introduction," exh. cat., October 16, 1991, Mary Ryan Gallery, New York.

1992   Dionisio D. Martinez, "Tobi Kahn," *Organica Quarterly*, Spring 1992, p. 23.

Nancy Grimes, "Review," *Art News*, February 1992, pp. 131–132.

Dionisio D. Martinez, "Review," *Art Papers*, March/April 1992, p. 57.

1993   Judy Arginteanu, "Review," *Minneapolis Star-Tribune*, May 28, 1993.

Diane Lewis, "Abstract Meanings," *The Wichita Eagle*, February 27, 1993, pp. C1-4.

Holland Cotter, "Tobi Kahn," *The New York Times*, Weekend section, November 26, 1993.

Douglas Dreishpoon, "Introduction," exh. cat., February 1993, Litwin Gallery, Wichita, Kansas.

1994   Janet Koplos, "Review," *Art in America*, May 1994, pp. 120–121.

Ann Berman, "In Total Harmony," *Town & Country*, June 1994, p. 159.

1995   "Noted Artist Tobi Kahn Unveils Works for South Salem Synagogue Sanctuary," *The Lewisboro Ledger*, Lewisboro, New York, January 26, 1995, p. 12.

Robin Cembalest, "Painting His Way to Transcendence," *Forward*, February 3, 1995, p. 10.

"Tobi Kahn Commission Unveiled by JFC," *Antiques and The Arts Weekly*, February 17, 1995, p. 49.

Grace Glueck, "Kahn-Do Spirit," *The New York Observer*, October 23, 1995.

Francine Koslow Miller, "Review," *Artforum*, November 1995, pp. 94–95.

1996   Alison Schneider, "Religion and Modern Art Find Common Ground," *The Chronicle of Higher Education*, April 26, 1996, pp. B4–5.

Kerry Dwyer, "Kahn's Mindscapes Take Over Where Memory Leaves Off," *The South Advocate*, May 22, 1996, p. 13.

DESIGN

Elizabeth Finger

EDITORS

Nessa Rapoport and Douglas Dreishpoon

EDITORIAL COORDINATOR

Sharon Florin

PHOTOGRAPHY

Nicholas Walster

PRINTING

Dai Nippon Printing Company

COVER

Sido, 1989
cat. 19

FRONTISPIECE

Rigu-Saar, 1993
cat. 26

All photography by Nicholas Walster, ©1997 Tobi Kahn,
with the following exceptions:

Paul L. Alt: *Shalev*, p. 16
David Heald: *Iza II*, p. 19, cat. 2
John Parnell Photography: *Giro III*, p. 38, cat. 3
Charles Mayer: *Eyda*, pp. 58–59, cat. 37